수능 영어를 향한 가벼운 발걸음

# 맨 처음 수능 영어

## 주제별 독해

# 2

**정담서**
쥬기스 변형문제 출제위원
이화여대졸
현) 대치세정학원(송도)

**안치현**
쥬기스 운영진
EBS 변형문제(모자이크)
Ashland Univ.(Ohio)
현) Promise Tesol Director (St. Louis)
현) 오르다 영어
현) 열린아카데미
현) 아이클레버유학원 자문위원

**이건희**
현) 쥬기스(http://jugis.co.kr) 대표
맨처음 수능영어(영문법, 기본, 실력, 독해, 완성)
내공(중학영문법, 중학구문, 중학듣기, 중학단어) (다락원)
체크체크(천재교육) Grammar in(비상) 외 집필
instagram@gunee27

**서재교**
대전 스카이피아학원 대표
〈저서〉
내공 중학영어 듣기시리즈(다락원)
맨처음 수능 영어 독해 모의고사 10회(다락원)
EBS 수능 변형문제시리즈(모자이크)
결정적코치 대입실전편 9 10(한국 교육컨설턴트 협의회)
〈검토위원〉
맨처음 수능영문법(다락원)
리더스뱅크 3~9, 완자 중고등 VOCA PICK 1~3(비상교육)

**이연홍**
경북대 졸
맨처음 수능 영어 독해 모의고사 10회, 내공중학영어듣기(다락원)
EBS고난도변형문제(모자이크)
현) 대치퍼스트학원 (창원)
현) Rhee's English Class (창원)
현) 이타카 영어학원(김해율하)

# 맨처음 수능 영어 주제별 독해 2

**지은이** 정담서 안치현 서재교 이연홍 이건희
**펴낸이** 정규도
**펴낸곳** (주)다락원

**초판 1쇄 인쇄** 2022년 12월 26일
**초판 1쇄 발행** 2023년 1월 2일

**편집** 김민아
**디자인** 김나경, 정규옥
**영문 감수** Ted Gray

**다락원** 경기도 파주시 문발로 211
**내용문의** (02)736-2031 내선 504
**구입문의** (02)736-2031 내선 250~252
**Fax** (02)732-2037
**출판등록** 1977년 9월 16일 제 406-2008-000007호

**Photo Credits**
Nenad Nedomacki (p.15), Oscity (p.49),
Maximum Exposure PR (p.50), Boris15 (p.52),
Igor Bulgarin (p.56), dennizn (p.64), DenPhotos (p.75),
Gil C (p.76), Roman Babakin (p.94), photoyh (p.100)
/ www.shutterstock.com

**값 14,500원**
ISBN 978-89-277-8046-5 54740
　　　978-89-277-8044-1 54740(set)

**http://www.darakwon.co.kr**
다락원 홈페이지를 방문하시면 상세한 출판정보와 함께
동영상강좌, MP3자료 등 다양한 어학 정보를 얻으실 수 있습니다.

수능 영어를 향한 가벼운 발걸음

수능 영어

주제별 독해

2

다락원

# 맨처음 수능 영어 주제별 독해만의 장점!

🐾 모의고사 및 수능 기출 문제를 쉽게 공부할 수 있어요!

🐾 수능 빈출 소재 & 주제별 학습으로 수능 영어와 친해질 수 있어요!

🐾 주제별 다양한 배경지식과 풍부한 어휘로 수능 영어 독해력을 키울 수 있어요!

**❶ 주제 소개**
수능에 자주 나오는 주제에 대한 소개와
주제별 학습 방향을 제시합니다.

> QR코드를 스캔하면 지문에
> 해당하는 원어민 음성을 들
> 을 수 있습니다.

**❹ Reading Check**
Q에 해당하는 지문을 요약 및 구조화합니다. 주제별 전개
방식은 물론 지문에 대한 이해도를 높일 수 있습니다.

---

## UNIT 01 인물, 일화

○ 주제 소개 ─ 주로 유명인의 업적, 기억에 남는 일화, 신기한 경험을 다루는 분야로, 수능에서는 세부내용 파악(내용불일치)으로 가장 많이 출제되며, 그 다음이 글의 순서, 문장삽입 유형이다. 하지만 글의 제목, 어법, 어휘 유형으로도 이따금 출제되니 주제와 관련된 다양한 수능 유형 학습으로 준비해야 한다.

**Q** Halet Cambel에 대한 다음 글의 내용과 일치하지 않는 것은? [78%] 고2 6월 모의고사 변형

After earning her doctorate degree from the University of Istanbul in 1940, Halet Cambel fought continually for the advancement of archaeology. She helped preserve some of Turkey's most important archaeological sites near the Ceyhan River and established an outdoor museum at Karatepe. There, she dug up one of humanity's oldest known civilizations by discovering a Phoenician alphabet tablet. Her work preserving Turkey's cultural heritage won her a Prince Claus Award. But she also dealt firmly with the political atmosphere of her time as well as revealed the secrets of the past. As just a 20-year-old archaeology student, Cambel went to the 1936 Berlin Olympics and became the first Muslim woman to compete in the Games. She was later invited to meet Adolf Hitler but she rejected the offer on political reasons.

① 고고학의 발전을 위해 끊임없이 애썼다.
② Karatepe에 야외 박물관을 건립했다.
③ 터키 문화 유산 보존으로 Prince Claus상을 받았다.
④ 올림픽에 참가한 최초의 무슬림 여성이다.
⑤ Adolf Hitler의 초대를 수락했다.

| New Words | | | | | |
|---|---|---|---|---|---|
| doctorate (degree) | 박사 학위 | site | 장소, 현장 | firmly | 확실히, 철저히 |
| degree | 학위 | establish | 건립[설립]하다 | political | 정치적인 |
| advancement | 발전 | dig up | 발굴하다 | reason | 이유, 추론하다 |
| preserve | 보전[보존]하다 | civilization | 문명 | atmosphere | 분위기, 대기 |
| archaeological | 고고학적인 | deal with | 다루다 | reveal | 드러내다, 밝히다 |

---

### Reading Check

빈칸에 들어갈 알맞은 말을 지문에서 찾아 적어 보세요.

| 주제 | • A life story about Halet Cambel |
|---|---|
| 인물 소개 | • Halet Cambel devoted herself to the advancement of ¹_____ |
| 활동 | • _____ a Phoenician alphabet tablet, from one of humanity's oldest ²_____<br>• was the first Muslim woman to _____ in the Olympic Games<br>• didn't accept the invitation from Adolf Hitler because of her _____ stance. |

### Analyzing Sentences

❶ She helped preserve some of Turkey's most important archaeological sites near the Ceyhan River and established an outdoor museum at Karatepe.
→ help가 3형식 동사일 때 목적어 자리에 원형부정사(preserve)와 to부정사(to preserve)를 모두 취할 수 있다. 동사는 목적어 또는 보어 자리에 무엇을, 어떤 형태로 취할 수 있는지를 결정하는 역할을 한다. help가 5형식 동사일 때도 목적격 보어 자리에 원형부정사와 to부정사를 모두 쓸 수 있다.

❷ But she also dealt firmly with the political atmosphere of her time as well as revealed the secrets of the past.
→ atmosphere가 '대기, 공기'가 아닌 '분위기'라는 뜻으로 쓰였다. B as well as A = not only A but also B로 'A뿐 아니라 B 역시'의 의미로 as well as는 뒤에서 앞으로 해석된다. A(revealed)와 B(dealt with)는 같은 동사 형태로 병렬 구조를 이루고 있다.

**Background Knowledge** 페니키아 알파벳(Phoenician alphabet)
유네스코 세계기록유산으로 일파벳의 원형이다. 당시 강대국인 이집트의 페소포타미아의 글자 체계를 사용하던 페니키아인들은 그리스문자들을 이용하여 페니카아 알파벳을 만들었다. 래머로의 한 사상가가 오늘날의 디지털 발명품들도 일파벳이 없었다면 발명되지 못했을 것이라 말했들이 모든 분야를 통틀어 가장 영향력 미친 발명품이다.

---

**❷ Q**
난이도를 조절한 기출 문제를 통해 수능 대표 주제에 대한
이해도를 높일 수 있습니다.

**❺ Analyzing Sentences**
지문 속 중요 구문이나 복잡한 문장 구조를
분석해보면서 문장 해석의 정확도를 높입니다.

**❸ New Words**
지문에 나온 단어들을 문제별로 정리했습니다. 영어 단어
와 한글 뜻을 스스로 체크해 볼 수 있는 깔끔한 단 구성은
단어 암기의 효율을 높여줍니다.

**❻ Background Knowledge**
주제별로 다양한 배경지식과 사진을 함께 보여줌으로써
보다 흥미롭고 생생한 독해를 할 수 있습니다.

## ❼ 주제별 연습문제
난이도에 맞게 변형된 기출 문제를 수능 빈출 소재와
주제별로 집중적으로 연습합니다.

정답률 및 기출문제 변형
정보를 알려줍니다.

## ❽ Vocabulary Review
주제별로 학습한 기출 지문 속 어휘들을
빈칸 완성, 영영 풀이를 통해 반복 학습합니다.

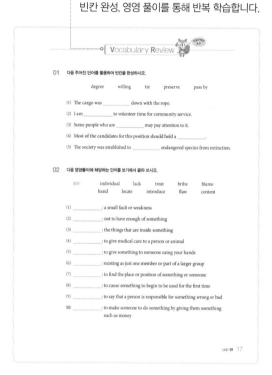

## ❾ ➕ (Expand Knowledge)
알아두면 유용한 다양한 배경지식을 사진과 함께
학습함으로써 주제에 대한 이해력과 독해력이 확장됩니다.

### MINI TEST
앞서 학습한 다양한
주제별 기출 문제들을
모의고사 형태의 미니
테스트를 통해 종합적
으로 점검해봅니다.

### • WORKBOOK
전 지문에 해당하는 핵심 어휘 및 구문 학습
용 워크북 문제를 제공합니다. 워크북 정답은
www.darakwon.co.kr에서 무료로 다운로
드 할 수 있습니다.

## 목차

책 속의 책 Workbook 제공

# 수능 영어 (절대평가)란 무엇인가요?

**기존의 상대평가와 달리 다른 학생의 성적과 비교하여 등급을 결정하지 않고,
본인의 성취 수준에 따라 등급을 결정합니다.**

## 1 수능 영어 문항과 시험 시간

수능 영어는 듣기와 읽기를 포함한 총 45문항으로 구성되어 있으며, 내용의 중요도나 난이도를 고려하여 문항별로 2점 또는 3점이 배정됩니다. 듣기 영역은 총 17문항으로서 듣기 12문항과 간접 말하기 5문항으로 구성되어 있습니다. 읽기 영역은 총 28문항으로서 읽기 21문항과 간접 쓰기 7문항으로 구성되어 있습니다. 시험 시간은 70분으로 듣기는 약 25분, 읽기는 약 45분이 배당되어 있습니다.

| 평가영역 | 문항수 | 시험시간 |
|---|---|---|
| 듣기 | 17문항 | 25분 |
| 읽기 | 28문항 | 45분 |
| 합계 | 45문항 | 70분 |

## 2 수능 영어 절대평가의 점수와 등급

수능 영어 절대평가는 원점수에 따른 등급만 제공합니다. 수능 영어 절대평가의 등급은 원점수 100점 만점을 기준으로 10점 간격의 9개 등급으로 구분됩니다. 예를 들어, 수험생이 90~100점 사이의 점수를 받으면 1등급, 80~89점 사이의 점수를 받으면 2등급을 받습니다.

| 성취등급 | 원점수 |
|---|---|
| 1등급 | 100~90점 |
| 2등급 | 89~80점 |
| 3등급 | 79~70점 |
| 4등급 | 69~60점 |
| 5등급 | 59~50점 |
| 6등급 | 49~40점 |
| 7등급 | 39~30점 |
| 8등급 | 29~20점 |
| 9등급 | 19~0점 |

## 3 수능 영어 평가 사항

수능 영어는 고등학교 영어 교육과정 성취기준의 달성 정도와 대학에서 수학하는 데 필요한 영어 능력을 평가하기 위한 시험입니다. 어법과 어휘, 글의 중심내용과 세부내용에 대한 문항, 논리적 관계 파악과 맥락 파악과 같은 글의 내용에 대한 이해력과 사고력 그리고 영어 표현을 상황에 맞게 사용하는 능력을 평가합니다.

## 4  수능 영어 읽기 학습

### ▮ 중심 내용 파악하기

중심 내용을 파악하기 위해서는 글을 읽고 전체적인 내용을 이해하고, 추론 하는 능력이 필요합니다. 중심 내용 파악하기에는 글의 주제, 요지, 제목 파악하기 등의 유형이 있습니다.

### ▮ 세부 내용 파악하기

세부 내용을 파악하기 위해서는 글에 제시된 특정 정보를 사실적이고 정확하게 이해하는 능력이 필요합니다. 세부 내용 파악하기에는 내용 일치·불일치, 실용문 및 도표 내용 일치·불일치 등 파악하기 유형이 있습니다.

### ▮ 논리적 관계 파악하기

논리적 관계를 파악하기 위해서는 글을 읽고 원인과 결과와 같은 내용의 논리적인 관계를 파악하는 능력이 필요합니다. 단어나 구, 절, 문장 또는 연결어가 들어갈 빈칸 내용 추론하기 등의 유형이 있습니다.

### ▮ 맥락 파악하기

맥락을 파악하기 위해서는 글을 읽고 말하는 이나 글쓴이의 의도나 목적을 파악하는 능력이 필요합니다. 맥락 파악하기에는 글쓴이의 목적, 주장, 글의 분위기나 심경 등 파악하기 등의 유형이 있습니다.

### ▮ 간접 쓰기

간접 쓰기를 위해서는 글의 전체적인 맥락과 문장 간의 논리적 흐름을 파악하여 가상의 글쓰기에 적용할 수 있는 능력이 필요합니다. 간접 쓰기에는 흐름에 무관한 문장, 주어진 문장의 적합한 위치, 글의 순서 파악하기, 문단 요약하기 등의 유형이 있습니다.

### ▮ 문법 및 어휘

문법 및 어휘를 위해서는 글의 전체적 의미나 문장 간의 의미적 관련성을 통하여 어법의 적합성이나 어휘의 적합성을 파악하는 능력이 필요합니다. 문법과 어휘에는 문맥에 따른 어법 또는 어휘 정확성 파악하기 등의 유형이 있습니다.

출처: 한국교육과정평가원

# 수능 지문의 6가지 대표 패턴

**Pattern 1** ▶ 주제문 ▶ 예시 ① ▶ 예시 ② ▶ 예시 ③

가장 기초적인 영어식 글쓰기 구성으로 「주제문+예시」의 기본 패턴입니다. 주제, 요지, 빈칸완성, 글의 전후 관계추론, 무관한 문장, 문장의 삽입 등 다양한 유형의 문제에 쓰입니다. 주제문은 문장 앞(두괄식), 문장 뒤(미괄식), 중간(중괄식), 혹은 앞과 뒤에 동시에 나올 수 있습니다. 예시를 위해 for example, for instance 같은 연결 어구를 사용합니다.

**Pattern 2** ▶ 도입 ▶ 주제문 ▶ 예시 ▶ 요약

수능에서 가장 많이 나오는 패턴으로 도입부에 일반적인 사실 또는 생각을 제시한 다음 but, however와 같이 역접을 유도하는 연결 어구를 사용하여 주제문을 제시합니다. 주제문을 보충 설명하기 위한 예를 2~3개 정도 쓰고 마지막에 전체 글을 요약합니다. 주로 주제, 요지, 주장, 빈칸 추론 등 유형에 활용합니다.

**Pattern 3** ▶ 일반론 ▶ 반론 ▶ 결론

논설문에서 가장 많이 쓰이는 형태입니다. 문장의 앞부분에 주제의 도입이나 일반적인 생각을 제시한 다음, 그와 반대되는 생각이나 문제점을 지적한 뒤 결론을 유도하는 방식입니다. 역접, 인과관계를 나타내는 연결 어구의 쓰임에 주의해야 합니다. 글의 순서 또는 문장의 삽입, 주제 등의 유형에서 많이 이용합니다.

**Pattern 4** ▶ 설명(사실 ① ② ③) ▶ 요약

설명문에서 많이 쓰이는 패턴으로, 주제를 정당화할 수 있는 사실, 속성, 사건들을 나열한 후 주제문을 제시합니다. 열거되는 사실은 서로 대등하며, first, second, finally, another, some, others 등을 사용합니다. 결론을 유도하는 therefore, in short 같은 접속부사의 표현을 글의 뒷부분에서 발견할 수 있습니다. 주로 실용문, 지칭추론, 빈칸 추론, 요지, 요약문 완성 등을 묻는 문제에 많이 응용됩니다.

**Pattern 5** ▶ 행동 ① ▶ 행동 ② ▶ 행동 ③

시간에 따른 어떤 대상의 움직임이나 장소를 구상하는 공간순서에 따른 행동에 대한 묘사로 어조, 분위기, 심경 또는 글의 순서 등을 파악하는 종합적인 이해력을 측정하는 문제에서 많이 활용합니다.

**Pattern 6** ▶ 상황 제시 ▶ 사건(시간순) ▶ 마무리

주제를 암시하는 사건을 시간 순으로 간략하게 서술합니다. 상황, 일화 등 사건의 흐름을 간결하게 서술하거나 글 속에 대화로 등장할 수 있습니다. 속담, 함축 의미, 심경을 묻거나 특히 장문 독해 문제에서 자주 활용합니다.

# 수능 주제별 독해

Unit 01 ~ Unit 16

주 제 소 개  주로 유명인의 업적, 기억에 남는 일화, 신기한 경험을 다루는 분야로, 수능에서는 세부내용 파악(내용불일치)으로 가장 많이 출제되며, 그 다음이 글의 순서, 문장삽입 유형이다. 하지만 글의 제목, 어법, 어휘 유형으로도 이따금 출제되니 주제와 관련된 다양한 수능 유형 학습으로 준비해야 한다.

**Q** Halet Cambel에 대한 다음 글의 내용과 일치하지 <u>않는</u> 것은?  74% 고2 06월 모의고사 변형

After earning her doctorate degree from the University of Istanbul in 1940, Halet Cambel fought continually for the advancement of archaeology. ❶She helped preserve some of Turkey's most important archaeological sites near the Ceyhan River and established an outdoor museum at Karatepe. There, she dug up one of humanity's oldest known civilizations by discovering a Phoenician alphabet tablet. Her work preserving Turkey's cultural heritage won her a Prince Claus Award. ❷But she also dealt firmly with the political atmosphere of her time as well as revealed the secrets of the past. As just a 20-year-old archaeology student, Cambel went to the 1936 Berlin Olympics and became the first Muslim woman to compete in the Games. She was later invited to meet Adolf Hitler but she rejected the offer on political reasons.

① 고고학의 발전을 위해 끊임없이 애썼다.
② Karatepe에 야외 박물관을 건립했다.
③ 터키 문화 유산 보존으로 Prince Claus상을 받았다.
④ 올림픽에 참가한 최초의 무슬림 여성이다.
⑤ Adolf Hitler의 초대를 수락했다.

**New Words**

| | | | | | |
|---|---|---|---|---|---|
| ☐ doctorate (degree) | 박사 학위 | ☐ site | 장소, 현장 | ☐ firmly | 확실히, 확고히 |
| ☐ degree | 학위 | ☐ establish | 건립[설립]하다 | ☐ political | 정치적인 |
| ☐ advancement | 발전 | ☐ dig up | 발굴하다 | ☐ reason | 이유; 추론하다 |
| ☐ preserve | 보존[보호]하다 | ☐ civilization | 문명 | ☐ atmosphere | 분위기, 대기 |
| ☐ archaeological | 고고학적인 | ☐ deal with | 다루다 | ☐ reveal | 드러내다, 밝히다 |

## Reading Check

빈칸에 들어갈 알맞은 말을 지문에서 찾아 적어 보세요.

| 주제 | • A life story about Halet Cambel |
|------|-----------------------------------|
| 인물 소개 | • Halet Cambel devoted herself to the advancement of ¹_____. |
| 활동 | • ²_____ a Phoenician alphabet tablet, from one of humanity's oldest ³_____<br>• was the first Muslim woman to ⁴_____ in the Olympic Games<br>• didn't accept the invitation from Adolf Hitler because of her ⁵_____ stance. |

## Analyzing Sentences

❶ She **helped preserve** some of Turkey's most important archaeological sites near the Ceyhan River and established an outdoor museum at Karatepe.

⋯⋯ help가 3형식 동사일 때 목적어 자리에 원형부정사(preserve)와 to부정사(to preserve)를 모두 취할 수 있다. 동사는 목적어 또는 보어 자리에 무엇을, 어떤 형태로 취할 수 있는지를 결정하는 역할을 한다. help가 5형식 동사일 때도 목적격 보어 자리에 원형부정사와 to부정사를 모두 쓸 수 있다.

❷ But she also **dealt** firmly **with** the political **atmosphere** of her time **as well as revealed** the secrets of the past.

⋯⋯ atmosphere가 '대기, 공기'가 아닌 '분위기'라는 뜻으로 쓰였다. B as well as A = not only A but also B로 'A뿐 아니라 B 역시'의 의미로 as well as는 뒤에서 앞으로 해석된다. A(revealed)와 B(dealt with)는 같은 동사 형태로 병렬 구조를 이루고 있다.

---

**Background Knowledge**

**페니키아 알파벳(Phoenician alphabet)**

유네스코 세계기록유산으로 알파벳의 원형이다. 당시 강대국인 이집트와 메소포타미아의 글자 체계를 사용하던 페니키아인들은 그리스문자를 이용하여 페니키아 알파벳을 만들었다. 레바논의 한 사상가가 오늘날의 디지털 발명품들도 알파벳이 없었다면 발명되지 못했을 것이라 말했듯이 모든 분야를 통틀어 가장 영향을 미친 발명품이다.

# 01

**다음 빈칸에 들어갈 말로 가장 적절한 것은?**   83% 고2 11월 모의고사 지문/문제 변형

A father took his son to the circus. Before the show started, he decided to see with his son the animals in their individual cages — all except for the elephant, which was tied with a rope. As the little boy was holding his father's hand, the little boy turned to him and said, "Dad, this elephant looks so huge and strong. He can kick the rope and run away. Why doesn't he?" No matter how hard he tried to think of a wise answer, the father didn't have a good one to give his son. So, he suggested to his son that he should go ask the question to the elephant trainer. When the boy saw the trainer passing by, he asked why the beast didn't try to get away. The trainer said, "When this elephant was a baby, we lashed the same rope to his foot and the tree. The elephant couldn't break free, and over time, he simply _____."

*lash 묶다

① came back on its own
② accepted the rope as a way of life
③ is looking forward to being free someday
④ is used to protecting himself from getting hurt
⑤ got to realize that it was safer to be managed by humans than in the wild

➕ **동춘서커스**
우리나라 최초의 서커스단으로 1952년에 동춘 박동수가 창설하여 2010년까지 약 85년 간 전통을 이어왔다. 전국을 떠돌며 공연하였고 1960~70년대에 전성기를 맞아 공연단원이 250명이 넘는 시절도 있었다. 동춘서커스단은 경영난에 시달려 해체를 결심한 적도 있으나 주변의 도움으로 위기를 이겨내며 현재도 그 명맥을 이어오고 있다.

**New Words**

| | | | | | |
|---|---|---|---|---|---|
| ☐ individual | 각각의, 개개의 | ☐ huge | 큰, 거대한 | ☐ trainer | 조련사 |
| ☐ tie | 묶다 | ☐ turn to | 돌아보다 | ☐ pass by | 지나가다 |
| ☐ hold | 잡다, 쥐다 | ☐ escape | 탈출하다; 탈출 | ☐ beast | 동물, 짐승 |
| ☐ run[get] away | 도망가다 | ☐ suggest | 제안하다, 시사하다 | ☐ break free | 탈출하다 |

55% 고2 09월 모의고사 지문/문제 변형

# 02

**Alexander the Great에 대한 다음 글의 내용과 일치하지 <u>않는</u> 것은?**

On his march through Asia Minor, Alexander the Great became dangerously ill. His physicians were afraid to treat him because if they didn't succeed, the army would blame them. Only one, Philip, was willing to take the risk, because he had confidence in the king's friendship and his own drugs. While the medicine was being prepared, Alexander received a letter saying that the physician had been bribed to poison his master. Alexander read the letter without showing it to anyone. When Philip entered the tent with the medicine, Alexander took the cup from him, handing Philip the letter. While the physician was reading it, Alexander calmly drank the contents of the cup. Extremely terrified, he threw himself down at the king's bedside, but Alexander told him that he completely trusted him. After three days, the king was well enough to appear again before his army.

① 대부분의 의사들은 Alexander의 치료에 실패할까 두려워했다.
② 의사인 Philip은 Alexander를 독살하라는 협박을 받고 치료를 거부했다.
③ Alexander는 Philip을 고발하는 내용의 편지를 받았음에도 약을 받아 마셨다.
④ Philip을 믿고 치료를 받은 Alexander는 회복하여 그의 군대로 복귀할 수 있었다.
⑤ Philip이 Alexander를 치료한 이유는 대왕과의 우정에 대한 믿음이 확고했기 때문이었다.

➕ **알렉산드로스 3세 대왕(Alexander the Great)**
고대 마케도니아 왕국의 왕으로 페르시아, 이집트를 정복하여 고대 그리스 역사상 가장 넓은 영토를 개척하였고 이로 인해 세계시민 사상인 헬레니즘 문화가 탄생했다. 영어 이름인 알렉산더 대왕으로 유명한 그는 키가 152cm인 작은 거인으로 아리스토텔레스의 제자이기도 하다.

**New Words**

| | | | | | |
|---|---|---|---|---|---|
| ☐ march | 진군; 행군하다 | ☐ take a risk | 위험을 감수하다 | ☐ hand | 건네다; 손 |
| ☐ physician | 의사, 내과의사 | ☐ confidence | 자신감 | ☐ calmly | 차분히, 조용히 |
| ☐ treat | 치료하다, 취급하다 | ☐ prepare | 준비[대비]하다 | ☐ content | 내용(물); 만족하는 |
| ☐ blame | 비난하다 | ☐ bribe | 뇌물을 주다; 뇌물 | ☐ terrified | 겁에 질린, 무서워하는 |
| ☐ willing | 기꺼이 ~하는 | ☐ poison | 독살하다; 독 | ☐ appear | 나타나다 |

## 03 주어진 글 다음에 이어질 글의 순서로 가장 적절한 것은?

82% 수능 지문/문제 변형

The Atitlán Giant Grebe was a large, flightless bird. By 1965 there were only around 80 birds left on Lake Atitlán.

(A) But there were other problems. An American airline was interested in developing the lake as a tourist destination for fishermen. However, there was a major problem with this idea: the lake lacked any suitable sporting fish!

(B) To solve this obvious flaw, a specially selected species of fish called the Large-mouthed Bass was introduced. The large-mouthed Bass instantly started to eat up the crabs and small fish that lived in the lake, thus competing with the few remaining grebes for food. It is also certain that the Large-mouthed Bass sometimes hunted the Atitlán Giant Grebe's chicks.

(C) One direct reason was easy enough to see: the local people were cutting down the reeds at a rapid rate. This destruction was caused by the needs of a fast growing mat-making industry.

*reed 갈대

① (A) – (C) – (B)　　　② (B) – (A) – (C)　　　③ (B) – (C) – (A)
④ (C) – (A) – (B)　　　⑤ (C) – (B) – (A)

➕ **외래종 부레옥잠**(water hyacinth, Eichhornia)
남아메리카의 수생식물로 엄청난 번식 속도로 수면을 빠르게 덮어 수중으로 들어가는 빛을 차단하여 생태계를 교란시키고 물을 썩게 만들어 최악의 외래종으로 꼽히고 있다. 하지만 한국에서는 추운 겨울로 인해 한철 식물이 되어 문제가 되지 않고 있다. 부레옥잠처럼 우리나라에 정착했다가 점차 개체가 줄어든 생물로는 황소개구리와 뉴트리아가 있다.

New Words

| □ flightless | 날지 못하는 | □ lack | ~이 없다[부족하다] | □ eat out | 먹어치우다 |
| □ locate | 알아내다, 찾아내다 | □ suitable | 적절한 | □ compete | 경쟁하다 |
| □ reed bed | 갈대밭 | □ flaw | 결함 | □ chick | 새끼 새, 병아리 |
| □ rate | 속도, 비율 | □ introduce | 도입하다 | □ direct | 직접적인 |
| □ tourist destination | 관광지 | □ instantly | 즉각, 즉시 | □ destruction | 파괴 |

**01** 다음 주어진 단어를 활용하여 빈칸을 완성하시오.

degree　　　willing　　　tie　　　preserve　　　pass by

(1) The cargo was ＿＿＿＿＿＿ down with the rope.

(2) I am ＿＿＿＿＿＿ to volunteer time for community service.

(3) Some people who are ＿＿＿＿＿＿ may pay attention to it.

(4) Most of the candidates for this position should hold a ＿＿＿＿＿＿.

(5) The society was established to ＿＿＿＿＿＿ endangered species from extinction.

**02** 다음 영영풀이에 해당하는 단어를 보기에서 골라 쓰시오.

보기　　　individual　　　lack　　　treat　　　bribe　　　blame
　　　　　hand　　　locate　　　introduce　　　flaw　　　content

(1) ＿＿＿＿＿＿: a small fault or weakness

(2) ＿＿＿＿＿＿: not to have enough of something

(3) ＿＿＿＿＿＿: the things that are inside something

(4) ＿＿＿＿＿＿: to give medical care to a person or animal

(5) ＿＿＿＿＿＿: to give something to someone using your hands

(6) ＿＿＿＿＿＿: existing as just one member or part of a larger group

(7) ＿＿＿＿＿＿: to find the place or position of something or someone

(8) ＿＿＿＿＿＿: to cause something to begin to be used for the first time

(9) ＿＿＿＿＿＿: to say that a person is responsible for something wrong or bad

(10) ＿＿＿＿＿＿: to make someone to do something by giving them something
　　　　　such as money

# UNIT 02 철학, 종교

**주 제 소 개**  인문학의 핵심이라고 할 수 있는 철학과 종교에 관련된 주제를 다루고 있다. 철학과 종교의 사회적 기능과 인간의 본성, 물질세계와 정신세계의 차이점과 유사점 등에 관한 내용이 주로 출제된다. 주로 빈칸 완성, 함의 추론, 흐름에 무관한 문장 찾기 등과 같은 논리 추론형 문제가 출제된다. 난이도가 높은 경우가 많으니, 소재의 흐름을 따라가며 읽는 연습이 필요하다.

---

**Q**  다음 빈칸에 들어갈 말로 가장 적절한 것은?  81% 고1 11월 모의고사 변형

Scottish economist Adam Smith saw competitiveness as maximizing self-interest. ❶He described the pursuit of self-interest and competitiveness as qualities that guide the economy. However, today the most 'competitive people' are replacing his philosophy with the thinking of the mathematician, John Nash. He proved mathematically the theory of Swiss philosopher Jean-Jacques Rousseau; when parties work together, the overall size of benefit almost always expands, so each party gets more than it could get alone. For example, four hunters can catch only one rabbit each when they act alone, but they can catch a deer when they do together. ❷So, today, smart competitors cooperate whenever they can. Research shows that almost 90 percent of the time, people in cooperative environments perform better than people in traditional, 'competitive,' win-lose environments. In other words, _____.

① collaboration produces better results
② overworking is a main cause of stress
③ cooperation doesn't reduce working hours
④ competition is necessary in the marketplace
⑤ many jobs require the ability to work independently

**New Words**

| | | | | | |
|---|---|---|---|---|---|
| □ economist | 경제학자 | □ quality | 자질 | □ overall size | 전체 크기 |
| □ competitiveness | 경쟁 | □ replace A with B | A를 B로 대체하다 | □ benefit | 이익; 이익을 주다 |
| □ maximize | 극대화하다 | □ mathematically | 수학적으로 | □ expand | 커지다, 확대되다 |
| □ self-interest | 자기 이익 | □ philosopher | 철학자 | □ cooperative | 협력하는 |
| □ pursuit | 추구 | □ party | 집단 | □ collaboration | 협업 |

정답과 해설
P.3

## Reading Check

빈칸에 들어갈 알맞은 말을 지문에서 찾아 적어 보세요.

| 도입 | Adam Smith<br>• The pursuit of ¹_____ self-interest and competition benefits the ²_____ as a whole. |
|---|---|
| 전개<br>(반박) | Jean-Jacques Rousseau<br>• The size of the benefit when working ³_____ is greater than that from working ⁴_____.<br>• Four hunters each can catch a rabbit, but if they work together, they can catch a deer. |
| 발전<br>(결론) | • People who ⁵_____ perform better than people who ⁶_____.<br>• Collaboration creates ⁷_____ results. |

## Analyzing Sentences

❶ He **described** the pursuit of self-interest and competitiveness **as qualities** [that guides the economy].

⋯▶ describe A as B의 구문으로 'A를 B로 설명하다[묘사하다]'는 의미이다. [ ]는 qualities를 수식하는 주격 관계대명사절이다.

❷ So, today, smart competitors cooperate [**whenever** they can].

⋯▶ [ ]에서 whenever는 '~할 때마다'의 의미로 부사절을 이끌며, 「every time 주어+동사」로 바꿔 쓸 수 있다. can 뒤의 생략된 동사는 cooperate로 문장 속에서 의미를 파악할 수 있는 경우 중복을 피하기 위해 생략한다.

---

**Background Knowledge**

### John Nash와 Game Theory

미국의 수학자인 John Nash는 게임이론으로 1994년 노벨경제학상을 수상하였다. 각 참가자들이 주어진 상황에서 최선의 선택을 함에도 불구하고 자신만의 이익을 고려한 선택으로 자신뿐만 아니라 상대방에게도 나쁜 결과를 야기한다는 죄수의 딜레마(Prisoner's Dilemma)가 대표적이다. Adam Smith의 '보이지 않는 손'의 원리와 반대되는 이론으로 사익의 극대화가 서로에게 손해가 될 수 있다는 것을 보여준다.

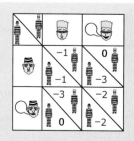

## 01 글의 흐름으로 보아, 주어진 문장이 들어가기에 가장 적절한 곳은?

60% 고2 11월 모의고사 변형

> In this perspective, people aren't cold theorizers who are making judgments about other creatures.

Philosophers have long argued about how people understand one another. Some believe that we carefully form a theory. ( ① ) We come up with hypotheses about how other people will behave, and then test those hypotheses against the evidence we observe minute by minute. ( ② ) In this theory, people constantly weigh evidence and test explanations, giving the impression that they are rational scientists. ( ③ ) And there's clear evidence that this sort of hypothesis testing is part of how we understand one another. ( ④ ) But these days most believe that one automatically puts him/herself in others' shoes, and understands what others feel by feeling what they are experiencing, within him/herself. ( ⑤ ) They are unconscious actors who understand by sharing or at least simulating the responses they see in the people around them.

**➕ 공감과 모사이론**

공감(empathy)은 "타인의 감정과 기분을 이해하기 위해 다른 사람의 입장에서 생각해보는 능력"이다. 심리학자 Theodor Lipps는 타인의 마음에 대한 이해는 상대방의 마음을 모방하는 것, 곧 '공감'에 있다고 보았다. 1980년대의 모사이론(Simulation Theory)은 타인의 상황에 자신을 투사한 후 자신의 심적 상태를 상상하고, 이를 타인에게 투사해보면서 마음 상태를 예측하고 추론할 수 있다고 보았다.

New Words

| | | | | | |
|---|---|---|---|---|---|
| ☐ perspective | 관점 | ☐ hypothesis | 가설 | ☐ explanation | 설명 |
| ☐ theorizer | 이론가 | ☐ behave | 행동하다 | ☐ impression | 인상 |
| ☐ judgment | 판단 | ☐ evidence | 증거 | ☐ rational | 이성적인 |
| ☐ argue | 논쟁하다 | ☐ observe | 관찰하다 | ☐ in others' shoes | ～의 입장에서 |
| ☐ one another | 서로 | ☐ minute by minute | 시시각각으로 | ☐ unconscious | 무의식적인 |
| ☐ carefully | 신중하게 | ☐ constantly | 끊임없이 | ☐ simulate | 흉내 내다 |
| ☐ come up with | 생각해 내다 | ☐ weigh | 따져 보다 | ☐ response | 반응 |

# 02

**다음 빈칸에 들어갈 말로 가장 적절한 것은?**   57% 고2 04월 모의고사 변형

Before his death, the contemporary Buddhist teacher Dainin Katagiri wrote a remarkable book called *Returning to Silence.* Life, he wrote, "is a dangerous situation." It is the weakness of life that makes it precious; his words are filled with the very fact of his own life passing away. "The china bowl is beautiful on the grounds that it will, someday, break.... The life of the bowl is always under dangerous circumstances." Our struggle for life is like that: our life is full of these kinds of inevitable wounds and unstable beauty. We forget — how easily we forget — that love and loss are intimate companions, and that we love the real flower so much more than the plastic one and love the cast of twilight across a mountainside lasting only a moment. It is this very _____ that opens our hearts.

① fragility ② stability ③ harmony
④ satisfaction ⑤ diversity

➕ 선불교(Zen Buddhism)
20세기 초 일본의 승려들이 최초로 선불교를 전파함에 따라, 선(禪)의 일본식 발음인 Zen(젠)으로 알려진 선불교는 한국, 중국, 일본을 중심으로 시작한 불교의 한 종파이나, 미국에서는 명상(meditation)을 배우려는 사람들을 중심으로 유행하였다.

New Words

| □ contemporary | 현대의 | □ china bowl | 도자기 그릇 | □ intimate | 친밀한 |
| □ Buddhist | 불교의 | □ on the grounds | ~라는 이유로 | □ companion | 동반자 |
| □ remarkable | 주목할 만한 | □ circumstance | 상황 | □ cast | 색조 |
| □ weakness | 연약함 | □ struggle | 투쟁 | □ twilight | 황혼 |
| □ precious | 소중한 | □ inevitable | 피할 수 없는 | □ mountainside | 산중턱 |
| □ pass away | 사망하다, 죽다 | □ unstable | 불안정한 | □ fragility | 연약함 |

# 03

**다음 글의 주제로 가장 적절한 것은?**

82% 고3 09월 모의고사 변형

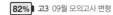

Influenced by philosophers from Plato to Descartes, conventional wisdom in the West says that individuals (especially geniuses) have creativity and originality. Social and cultural influences and causes are ignored or completely eliminated from consideration. Thoughts, whether original or conventional, are identified with individuals, and the special things they do are attributed to their genes and their brains. The "trick" here is to recognize that individual humans are social constructions themselves, embodying and reflecting the variety of social and cultural influences they have been exposed to during their lives. That is, our individuality is not denied, but viewed as a product of specific social and cultural experiences. The brain itself is a social thing, influenced structurally and at the level of its connectivities by social environments. The "individual" is legal, religious, and political fiction just as the "I" is a grammatical illusion.

① recognition of the social nature inherent in individuality
② ways of filling the gap between individuality and collectivity
③ issues with separating original thoughts from conventional ones
④ acknowledgment of the true individuality embodied in human genes
⑤ necessity of shifting from individualism to interdependence

**➕ 모글리 현상(Mowgli Syndrome)**
영국의 작가 J.R 커플링의 동화 '정글북'에 등장하는 늑대에 의해 길러진 모글리처럼 현실세계에서 야생동물에 의해 길러진 아이들이 야생동물과 같이 행동하는 것을 말한다. 이 현상은 사람의 인간다움은 타고나는 것이 아니라 사회화(socialization)의 과정을 통해 형성된다는 것을 보여주는 한 사례이다.

New Words

| | | | | | |
|---|---|---|---|---|---|
| ☐ conventional | 관습적인 | ☐ embody | 구현하다 | ☐ connectivity | 연결성 |
| ☐ originality | 독창성 | ☐ variety | 다양성 | ☐ religious | 종교적인 |
| ☐ identify with | ~와 동일시하다 | ☐ deny | 부인하다 | ☐ fiction | 허구 |
| ☐ be attributed to | ~에 기인하다 | ☐ be viewed as | ~로 여겨지다 | ☐ grammatical | 문법적인 |
| ☐ gene | 유전자 | ☐ specific | 특정한 | ☐ illusion | 환상 |

**01** 다음 주어진 단어를 활용하여 빈칸을 완성하시오.

| impression | competitiveness | response | inevitable | originality |

(1) She didn't have a chance to show her artistic _____.

(2) Brains have to keep track of hundreds of different _____ to thousands of stimuli.

(3) The development of new cars has heightened _____ between the manufacturers.

(4) Because our feelings of superiority could not be sustained, we experienced an _____ fall.

(5) Keep in mind that, to leave a good _____, your "good-bye" must be bigger than your "hello."


**02** 다음 영영풀이에 해당하는 단어를 보기에서 골라 쓰시오.

보기　contemporary　cooperative　specific　fiction　struggle
　　　expand　conventional　hypothesis　rational　perspective

(1) _____: something that is not true

(2) _____: clearly and exactly presented or stated

(3) _____: happening or beginning now or in recent times

(4) _____: a way of thinking about and understanding something

(5) _____: to increase in size, range, or amount to become bigger

(6) _____: based on facts or reason and not on emotions or feelings

(7) _____: been around for a long time and is considered to be typical

(8) _____: a theory that is not proven but that leads to further study

(9) _____: a long effort to do or achieve something that causes problems

(10) _____: involving two or more people working together to do something

# 03 역사, 풍습, 지리

**UNIT**

주 제 소 개    역사적 사건, 풍습, 지리적 특성과 관련된 흥미로운 이야기, 또는 유래 등을 통해 존재하지만 잘 알려지지 않거나 잘못 알려진 것들, 관심이 필요한 내용에 관한 이야기가 주로 다루어진다. 글의 순서, 문장 삽입, 요약하기 등의 수능 유형으로 주로 출제된다.

**Q**    **다음 글에서 전체 흐름과 관계 없는 문장은?**    `69%` 고2 11월 모의고사 변형

Back in the seventeenth century, hair had a special spiritual meaning in Africa. ❶Many African cultures saw the head as the center of control, communication, and identity in the body. ① Hair was considered a source of power, and people also thought that the power of hair could cause the individual to exist, and that could also be used for spiritual purposes or even for a magic. ② Because it is on the highest point on the body, hair itself was a way to communicate with divine spirits. ❷Besides, it was thought that hair could bring good luck or protect against evil. ③ People had the opportunity to socialize while styling each other's hair, and the shared tradition of hair was passed down. ④ According to authors Ayana Byrd and Lori Tharps, "communication from the gods and spirits was thought to pass through the hair to get to the soul." ⑤ In Cameroon, for example, medicine men put hair to boxes that contained their healing potions in order to protect the potions and  increase their effectiveness.

*potion (마법의) 물약

**New Words**

| | | | | | |
|---|---|---|---|---|---|
| □ spiritual | 영적인 | □ communicate | 의사소통하다 | □ pass down | ~을 전해주다 |
| □ center | 중심 | □ divine | 신성한, 신의 | □ medicine man | 치료 주술사 |
| □ identity | 정체성 | □ spirit | 정신, 영혼 | □ contain | 담다, 들어 있다 |
| □ source | 원천 | □ socialize | 사귀다, 사회화하다 | □ protect | 보호하다 |
| □ see A as B | A를 B로 여기다 | □ style | (스타일을) 만들다 | □ effectiveness | 효과 |

## Reading Check

빈칸에 들어갈 알맞은 말을 지문에서 찾아 적어 보세요.

| 주제 | A special ¹_____ meaning of hair in Africa |
|------|----------------------------------------------------|
| 머리카락에 대한 인식 | Hair is considered ~. <br>• the ²_____ of control, communication, and identity in the body <br>• a source of ³_____ <br>• the power of hair causes the individual to ⁴_____ <br>• to ⁵_____ good luck or ⁶_____ against evil. |

## Analyzing Sentences

**❶** Many African cultures **saw** the head **as** the center of control, communication, and identity in the body.

⋯▸ see A as B는 'A를 B라고 여기다'라는 구문으로, see 대신에 view, regard, think of, deem A as B로도 쓸 수 있다.

**❷** Besides, **it was thought that** hair could bring good luck or protect against evil.

⋯▸ It is though that은 '~라고 여겨지다'의 뜻으로 'Hair was thought to be able to bring good luck or protect against evil.'로 바꿔 쓸 수 있다. Besides는 '게다가'라는 의미의 부사로 쓰였다. 전치사일 때는 '~이외에도'라는 뜻이다.

**Background Knowledge**

**우리나라 최초의 이발사 '안종호', 선구자 '오엽주'**
우리나라는 신체발부 수지부모(身體髮膚 受之父母)라고 부모에게 받은 머리카락을 소중히 여겼다. 하지만 1895년 갑오개혁 이후 단발령이 내려졌고, 안종호는 본인의 상투를 자르고 대한제국 왕실 최초의 이발사가 되었다. 또한 오엽주는 우리나라 미용계의 선구자로 최초로 파마를 한 미용사이다. 파마는 그 당시 가부장적인 분위기 속에서 여성들의 의식구조를 바꿨다고 할 만큼 획기적인 것이었다.

## 01

**다음 빈칸에 들어갈 말로 가장 적절한 것은?** 57% 고2 09월 모의고사 지문/문제 변형

The major oceans are all interconnected, so that their geographical borders are more difficult to identify than those of the continents. Consequently, their biotas show fewer evident differences than those on land. The oceans themselves are continually moving because the water within each ocean basin slowly revolves. These moving waters carry marine organisms from place to place, and also help the distribution of their young or larvae. Furthermore, the gradients between the environments of different areas of ocean water mass are very progressive and often extend over wide areas that are inhabited by a great variety of organisms of differing ecological tolerances. There are _____ within the open oceans although there may be barriers to the movement of organisms.

*biota 생물 군집 **gradient 변화도 ***ocean basin 해저분지

① no firm boundaries
② limits of biodiversity
③ little territorial sea issues between countries
④ the evidence that the sea is freer than the continents
⑤ discussion of how the more species can spread to wider sea

**➕ 태평양 쓰레기섬(Garbage Patch)**
바다에 버려지는 쓰레기들이 북서태평양 한 곳에 모여 거대한 섬을 이룬 것으로 비닐과 플라스틱류가 90%가량 차지한다. 쓰레기들은 미세플라스틱으로 분해되는 등 사람은 물론 바다에 서식하는 생물들에게도 심각한 피해를 입힌다. 국가와 기업들은 해양쓰레기를 수거하는 오션클린업을 지원하고 있다.

**New Words**

| | | | | | |
|---|---|---|---|---|---|
| ☐ interconnected | 서로 연결된 | ☐ evident | 명백한 | ☐ progressive | 점진적인 |
| ☐ geographical | 지리적인, 지리의 | ☐ revolve | 회전하다 | ☐ inhabited | 서식하는 |
| ☐ border | 경계 | ☐ marine | 해양의 | ☐ ecological | 생태학적인 |
| ☐ identify | 식별하다, 확인하다 | ☐ distribution | 분포, 분배 | ☐ tolerance | 내성, 관용 |
| ☐ continent | 대륙 | ☐ larvae | 유충 | ☐ barrier | 방해물 |

## 02

다음 글의 주제로 가장 적절한 것은?

51% 고2 06월 모의고사 변형

The development of writing was pioneered by accountants, not by gossips, storytellers, or poets. The earliest writing system has its foundation in the Neolithic period, in which there was a significant change of the living; from hunting and gathering to a settled lifestyle based on agriculture. The region where this shift began, around 9500 B.C., was known as the Fertile Crescent, which stretches from modern-day Egypt up to southeastern Turkey, and down again to the border between Iraq and Iran. Writing appears to have evolved in this region from the practice of using small clay pieces to account for exchanges for agricultural goods such as grain, sheep, and cattle. The first written documents, from the Mesopotamian city of Uruk in around 3400 B.C., record amounts of bread, payment of taxes, and other transactions using simple symbols and marks on clay tablets.

*Neolithic period 신석기 시대 **transaction 거래

① various tools to improve agricultural production
② regional differences in using the writing system
③ ways to store agricultural goods in ancient cities
④ changed lifestyles based on agricultural development
⑤ early writing as a means of recording economic activities

➕ **지상의 문자 발상지 우루크(Uruk)**
고대 메소포타미아 지방에 존재했던 수메르 문명의 도시 국가 중 하나이다. 길가메시 왕이 우루크를 차지한 후 정복과 함락, 부흥을 반복하며 7세기에 완전히 사라졌다. 우루크 유적은 1849년 발굴되었으며 '이라크 남부의 아흐와르'라는 이름으로 유네스코 세계유산에 등재되었다.

New Words

| □ pioneer | 개척하다 | □ hunting | 수렵, 사냥 | □ appear | ~처럼 보이다 |
| □ accountant | 회계사 | □ gathering | 채집, 수확 | □ practice | 관습 |
| □ gossip | 수다쟁이, 험담꾼 | □ settled | 자리를 잡은, 안정된 | □ account for | ~을 설명하다 |
| □ poet | 시인 | □ shift | 변화 | □ cattle | 소(떼) |
| □ foundation | 근간, 기반, 토대 | □ border | 국경, 경계 | □ transaction | 거래 |
| □ significant | 엄청난, 중요한 | □ stretch | 뻗어 있다 | □ clay tablet | 점토판 |

## 03

다음 빈칸에 들어갈 말로 가장 적절한 것은?

38% 고3 06월 모의고사 변형

One striking aspect of aboriginal culture is the concept of "totemism," where the tribal member at birth assumes the soul and identity of a part of nature. This light of the earth and its fertility as a natural part of oneself clearly causes one to refrain from mistreatment of the environment because that would only mean a destruction of oneself. Totems are more than objects. They include spiritual rituals, word-of-mouth histories, and the ceremonial lodges where the records of the past travel routes of the soul exist and can be a mythology. The main motivation is the preservation of tribal myths and an integration and sharing of every individual's origins in nature. The aborigines see _____, through totems that connect to their ancestors, a cosmology that places them with the earth, and behavior patterns that respect ecological balance.

*aboriginal 원주민의

① themselves as incompatible with nature and her riches
② their mythology as a primary motive toward individualism
③ their identity as being self-contained from surrounding nature
④ their relationship to the environment as a single harmonious continuum
⑤ their communal rituals as a gateway to distancing themselves from their origins

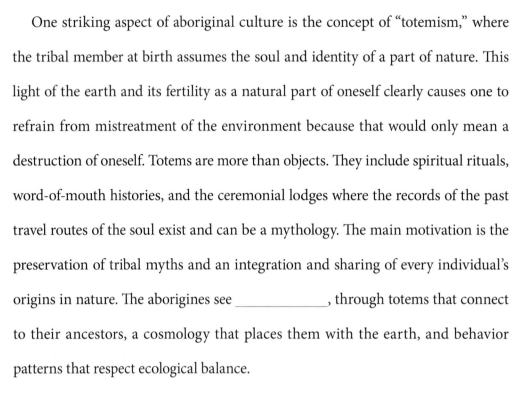

➕ 우리나라의 건국신화 – 단군신화
환웅이 인간 세상을 구하고자 했을 때 환인은 천부인(청동검·청동거울·청동방울)을 주어 홍익인간 정신을 실현하게 하였다. 사람이 되려면 쑥과 마늘을 100일간 먹어야 했는데, 호랑이는 포기하였으나 곰은 견뎌내 환웅과 결혼해 단군을 낳았다. 그 후 단군은 평양에 수도를 정하고 조선이라 칭했다.

New Words

| □ striking | 놀라운 | □ mistreatment | 학대 | □ preservation | 보존 |
| □ assume | 취하다, 띠다 | □ destruction | 파괴 | □ integration | 통합 |
| □ light | 관점, 견해 | □ word-of-mouth | 구전의 | □ continuum | 연속체 |
| □ fertility | 풍요, 비옥함 | □ lodge | 오두막 | □ cosmology | 우주론 |
| □ refrain from | ~을 삼가다, 절제하다 | □ mythology | 신화 (= myth) | □ respect | 존중하다 |

**01** 다음 주어진 단어를 활용하여 빈칸을 완성하시오.

> communicate     identify     pioneer     appear     assume

(1) They were able to _____ the criminal.

(2) I think that the figures _____ to be realistic.

(3) The phenomenon _____ great significance.

(4) I will _____ a highly innovative method of experiments.

(5) This is the means by which we _____ with one another.

**02** 다음 영영풀이에 해당하는 단어를 보기에서 골라 쓰시오.

> 보기     fertility     foundation     divine     distribution     practice
> integration     border     socialize     inhabited     shift

(1) _____ : sacred, holy, or godlike

(2) _____ : a change in position or direction

(3) _____ : the state or quality of being abundant

(4) _____ : to behave in a friendly or sociable manner

(5) _____ : a customary, habitual, or expected procedure

(6) _____ : living in a place, to have a home somewhere

(7) _____ : something that provides support for another thing

(8) _____ : the act of combining or adding parts to make a unified whole

(9) _____ : the way in which something is shared out or spread over an area

(10) _____ : a line separating one country from another or a boundary between places

# UNIT 04 물리, 화학, 항공우주

**주 제 소 개**　일상의 흔한 경험을 과학의 언어로 객관적이고 논증적으로 설명해주거나 획기적 발견 또는 물리, 화학, 우주 과학의 전망 등을 주로 다루고 있으며 정보 전달이 주된 목적이다. 수능에서는 글의 순서, 문장 삽입, 빈칸 완성 등의 유형으로 주로 출제된다.

---

60% 수능 지문/문제 변형

**Q** 다음 글의 내용을 한 문장으로 요약하고자 한다. 빈칸 (A), (B)에 들어갈 말로 가장 적절한 것은?

In physics, scientists develop models, or theories, to explain and predict the data we observe about the universe. Newton's theory of gravity is one example; Einstein's theory of gravity is another. Those theories, though they describe the same phenomenon, deal with very different versions of reality. ❶Newton, for example, imagined that masses affect each other by applying a force, while in Einstein's theory the effects occur through a bending of space and time, and there is no concept of gravity as a force. ❷Either theory could be used to describe the falling of an apple accurately, but Newton's would be much easier to use. On the other hand, for the calculations necessary for a GPS that helps you navigate while driving, Newton's theory would give the wrong answer, and so Einstein's must be used.

↓

| There are different views on an identical ___(A)___ in each scientist's theory, so the field that each theory ___(B)___ to may be different. |
|---|

|  | (A) |  | (B) |  | (A) |  | (B) |
|---|---|---|---|---|---|---|---|
| ① | side effect | ······ | conforms | ② | hypothesis | ······ | contributes |
| ③ | observation | ······ | submits | ④ | phenomenon | ······ | applies |
| ⑤ | demonstration | ······ | object |  |  |  |  |

---

New Words

| □ predict | 예측하다 | □ gravity | 중력 | □ either | 둘 중 하나 |
|---|---|---|---|---|---|
| □ observe | 관찰하다 | □ mass | 질량, 덩어리 | □ navigate | 길을 찾다, 항해하다 |
| □ universe | 우주 | □ apply | 적용하다 | □ identical | 동일한 |
| □ deal with | 다루다 | □ bending | 구부러짐 | □ phenomenon | 현상 |

정답과 해설 P.7

## Reading Check

빈칸에 들어갈 알맞은 말을 지문에서 찾아 적어 보세요.

| 주제 | Differing perspectives of scientists for the same [1]_____ |
|---|---|
| 비교 ① | **Newton's theory**<br>• [2]_____ affect each other by [3]_____ a force.<br>→ It would be easier to describe the [4]_____ of an apple. |
| 비교 ② | **Einstein's theory**<br>• Gravity occurs through a [5]_____ of space and time, not as a force.<br>→ It would help [6]_____ while driving with a GPS. |

## Analyzing Sentences

❶ Newton, for example, **imagined that** masses **affect** each other by applying a force, ~.
⋯▶ 일반적으로 종속절(that이하)의 시제는 본동사와 같거나 앞선 시제로 시제일치가 되어야 한다. 하지만 종속절의 내용이 일반적인 사실이거나, 불변의 진리 등일 경우 예외가 적용된다. Newton이 과거에 생각한 것이므로 과거시제(imagined)이지만 종속절의 내용은 이론의 내용이므로 현재시제(affect)가 쓰였다.

❷ Either theory could **be used to describe** the falling of an apple accurately, ~.
⋯▶ either는 '둘 중 하나'의 뜻이며,「be used to+동사원형」은 '~하는데 쓰이다'라는 뜻이다. 혼동하기 쉬운 구문으로는「be used to+동사원형-ing」'~하는데 익숙하다',「used to+동사원형」 '~하곤 했다'가 있다.

**Background Knowledge**

**페르디난드 마젤란의 항해 – 지구는 둥글다**

1519년 스페인에서 출발한 마젤란은 태평양을 건넌 최초의 유럽인이 되었다. 3년 1개월 걸친 세계일주에 성공한 탐험대원들은 1522년 9월 8일 귀환하여 지구가 둥글다는 것을 입증하였다. 266명 중 18명만이 살아남은 험난한 여정이었다. 마젤란은 여정 중 원주민과의 전투에서 죽었다고 알려졌다.

# 01

다음 글의 밑줄 친 부분 중, 문맥상 어법의 쓰임이 적절하지 <u>않은</u> 것은? [64%] 고2 04월 모의고사 지문/문제 변형

I was sitting outside a restaurant in Spain one summer evening, waiting for dinner. The scent of the kitchen stimulated my taste buds. The meal that I was expecting to have was coming to me in the form of molecules drifting through the air, too small for my eyes to see but ① <u>detected</u> by my nose. The ancient Greeks first came upon the idea of atoms this way; the smell of baking bread suggested to them that small particles of bread ② <u>existed</u> beyond vision. The cycle of weather reinforced this idea: a puddle of water on the ground gradually dries out, disappears, and then falls later as rain. They inferred ③ <u>what</u> there must be particles of water that turn into steam, form clouds, and fall to earth, so that the water is ④ <u>conserved</u> even though the little particles are too small to see. My paella in Spain had inspired me, four thousand years too ⑤ <u>late</u> to take the credit for atomic theory.

*taste bud 미뢰(혀의 미각기관) **molecule 분자 ***paella 파에야(스페인 요리의 하나)

Perfume

➕ 향기 마케팅

후각은 인간의 오감 가운데 기억과 감정에 연결된 유일한 감각기관이다. 인간의 감정 75%가 후각에 좌우될 정도로 영향력이 크다. 일본의 비누 회사가 신문 광고에 향기가 나도록 향료를 잉크에 섞어 인쇄한 것이 최초의 향기 마케팅이 되었다. 현재는 공간을 향으로 채워 고객의 소비를 유도하는 마케팅도 흔하게 이루어지고 있으며 브랜드, 심지어 공항도 시그니처 향기를 가지고 있다.

New Words

| | | | | | |
|---|---|---|---|---|---|
| ☐ wait for | ~을 기다리다 | ☐ particle | 입자 | ☐ conserve | 보존[보호]하다 |
| ☐ scent | 향기 | ☐ beyond vision | 눈에 보이지 않는 | ☐ inspire | 영감을 주다 |
| ☐ stimulate | 자극하다 | ☐ reinforce | 강화하다 | ☐ take the credit | 공로를 인정받다 |
| ☐ drift | 떠돌다, 이동하다 | ☐ infer | 추론하다 | ☐ atomic | 원자의 |
| ☐ detect | 감지하다 | ☐ steam | 수증기 | | |

## 02 다음 글에서 전체 흐름과 관계 <u>없는</u> 문장은?

Besides adjusting temperatures when handling fresh produce, control of the atmosphere is essential. ① While some moisture in the air prevents dehydration during storage, too much moisture can lead to growth of molds. ② Some commercial warehouses have controlled atmospheres, in which the levels of both carbon dioxide and moisture are modified carefully. ③ Though living things emit carbon dioxide when they breathe, carbon dioxide is widely considered to be a pollutant. ④ Sometimes other gases, such as ethylene gas, may be introduced at appropriate levels to help achieve an optimal quality of bananas and other fresh produce. ⑤ The need for some circulation of air among the stored foods is related to the control of gases and moisture.

*dehydration 탈수  **controlled atmosphere 저온 저장과 함께 공기의 농도를 조절하는 장치

➕ 홈파밍(Home farming)
코로나19, 경기 위축 등의 상황에서 홈파밍(집에서 채소를 직접 길러먹는 것) 열풍이 불고 있다. 식자재 부담을 줄이는 동시에 집에 머무는 시간이 많아진 요즘 취미생활의 영역까지 확대되었다. 대파, 바질, 상추 등의 식물 모종, 씨앗, 재배기 판매의 인기는 갈수록 증가하고 있다.

 New Words

| | | | | | |
|---|---|---|---|---|---|
| □ besides | ~이외에도 | □ lead to | ~로 이어지다, 야기하다 | □ breathe | 호흡하다 |
| □ adjust | 조절하다, 적응하다 | □ mold | 곰팡이 | □ pollutant | 오염 물질 |
| □ produce | 농산물; 생산하다 | □ warehouse | 저장 창고 | □ appropriate | 적절한, 적당한 |
| □ atmosphere | 공기, 대기, 분위기 | □ regulate | 규제하다 | □ introduce | 도입하다 |
| □ prevent | ~을 하지 못하게 하다 | □ modify | 조정[수정]하다 | □ optimal | 최적의 |
| □ storage | 저장 | □ emit | 방출하다 | □ circulation | 순환 |

# 03 주어진 글 다음에 이어질 글의 순서로 가장 적절한 것은?

53% 고3 06월 모의고사 지문/문제 변형

> Whispering galleries are astonishing acoustic spaces found beneath certain domes or curved ceilings.

(A) To realize this effect, the two of you should stand at diagonally opposite corners of the space, facing the wall. Now you are near a focus; a special point where the sound from you gets concentrated as it reflects off the curved walls and ceiling.

(B) A famous one is located outside a well-known restaurant in New York City's Grand Central Station. It's an intriguing place to take a date: the two of you can exchange romantic words while you're forty feet apart and separated by a congested passageway. You'll hear each other clearly, but the passersby won't hear what you're saying.

(C) Normally, the sound waves you make travel in all directions and bounce off the walls at different times and places, mixing them so much that they are not delivered to the ear of a listener forty feet away. But when you whisper at a focus, the reflected waves all arrive simultaneously at the other focus, thus reinforcing one another and allowing your words to be heard.

*acoustic 음향의 **diagonally 대각선으로

① (A) – (C) – (B)　　② (B) – (A) – (C)　　③ (B) – (C) – (A)
④ (C) – (A) – (B)　　⑤ (C) – (B) – (A)

**➕ 이글루(Igloo)의 과학적 원리**
이글루 내부 온도를 영상 5도로 유지할 수 있는 비법은 공기이다. 눈이 지닌 공기가 열이 빠져나가지 않게 한다. 추울수록 이글루 안에 물을 뿌리는데 물이 응고하며 열에너지가 발생하는 과학 원리를 이용한 것이다.

New Words

| □ astonishing | 놀라운 | □ intriguing | 흥미로운 | □ bounce off | ~에서 반사되다 |
| □ realize | 실현하다, 깨닫다 | □ congested | 혼잡한 | □ simultaneously | 동시에 |
| □ reflect | 반사하다 | □ passerby | 지나가는 사람 | □ reinforce | 강화하다 |

**01** 다음 주어진 단어를 활용하여 빈칸을 완성하시오.

| deal with | scent | adjust | conserve | apply |
|---|---|---|---|---|

(1) The room is filled with the _____ of flowers.

(2) He was about to _____ some common misconceptions.

(3) We are going to enact new laws to _____ wildlife in the area.

(4) They can _____ to changes in their environment to accomplish the goal.

(5) The G20 summit will _____ sanctions against countries that violate the international standards.

**02** 다음 영영풀이에 해당하는 단어를 보기에서 골라 쓰시오.

| 보기 | realize | modify | inspire | infer | reflect |
|---|---|---|---|---|---|
| | congested | drift | passerby | navigate | emit |

(1) _____ : to move slowly on water or wind

(2) _____ : to cause something to become real

(3) _____ : to make someone want to do something

(4) _____ : to send light or energy out from something

(5) _____ : to change something, in order to improve it

(6) _____ : to show the image of something on a surface

(7) _____ : a person who is walking past somebody by chance

(8) _____ : to reach a conclusion based on known facts or evidence

(9) _____ : too full or crowded with something such as vehicles or people

(10) _____ : to find the way to get to a place, traveling in a ship, an airplane, or a car

# 생명과학, 지구과학

**주 제 소 개**   신체와 지구 활동의 메커니즘(작동 원리와 구조)에 관련한 정보를 다룬다. 실생활에 밀접하게 연관된 생명과학, 지구과학에 대한 이야기를 통해 지식 전달과 함께 때로는 인간의 경각심을 불러일으키는 것을 목적으로 한다. 글의 주제, 함축적 의미 파악, 흐름에 무관한 문장 찾기 등의 수능 유형으로 주로 출제된다.

**Q**   글의 흐름으로 보아, 주어진 문장이 들어가기에 가장 적절한 곳은?   52% 고2 06월 모의고사 변형

> If this lasts for any length of time, the reactions in our cells cannot continue and we perish.

❶Wherever we go and whatever we do ❷the body temperature is maintained at the temperature at which our enzymes work best. It is not the temperature at the surface of the body that matters. ( ① ) It is the temperature deep inside the body which must be kept consistent. ( ② ) Our enzymes cannot be active at only a few degrees above or below normal body temperature. ( ③ ) All sorts of things can affect internal body temperature, from heat generated in the muscles during exercise, to fevers caused by disease, and to the external temperature. ( ④ ) There are lots of ways that we can adjust our temperature: by changing our clothing, the way we behave and the amount of our activities. ( ⑤ ) But we do also have an intrinsic regulation mechanism: when we get too hot we start to sweat.

\*enzyme 효소

**New Words**

| | | | | | |
|---|---|---|---|---|---|
| □ temperature | 온도 | □ matter | 중요하다 | □ adjust | 조절[조정]하다 |
| □ maintain | 유지하다 | □ surface | 표면 | □ behave | 행동하다 |
| □ last | 지속되다 | □ consistent | 일관된 | □ intrinsic | 타고난, 고유의 |
| □ length | 길이, 시간[기간] | □ internal | 내부의 | □ regulation | 통제, 규제 |
| □ reaction | 반응 | □ generate | 발생시키다 | □ sweat | 땀을 흘리다 |
| □ perish | 죽다, 소멸하다 | □ external | 외부의 | | |

빈칸에 들어갈 알맞은 말을 지문에서 찾아 적어 보세요.

| 주제 | The importance of maintaining internal body ¹_____ |
|------|------------------------------------------------------------|
| 체온 유지 | • It is ²_____ body temperature that matters.<br>　– has something to do with the function of ³_____<br>　– is affected by heat, fever, and external temperature<br>• ways to ⁴_____ our temperature:<br>　– not only by clothing but also by the activation of an ⁵_____ regulation mechanism |

### Analyzing Sentences

❶ [**Wherever** we go and **whatever** we do] the body temperature ~.

⋯→ [ ] 부분은 「관계사+ever」 형태인 복합관계사가 이끄는 양보 부사절로 쓰였다. 「no matter 의문사」로 바꿔 쓸 수 있다. 즉, 'No matter where we go and no matter what we do ~.'와 같은 문장이다.

❷ ~ the body temperature is maintained at **the temperature** [**at which** our enzymes work best].

⋯→ [ ] 부분은 the temperature를 꾸미는 형용사절로 'Our enzymes work best at temperature.'가 원래 문장이기 때문에 at which(= at temperature)이며 where로 바꿔 쓸 수 있다.

**Background Knowledge**

**수면 호르몬 – 멜라토닌과 세로토닌**

멜라토닌은 수면에 관여하는 호르몬으로 빛의 자극이 적을 때 분비된다. '검정색'이라는 뜻의 그리스어 '멜라스'와 신경전달물질인 '세로토닌'이 합쳐서 멜라토닌이 되었다. 체온이 낮아져야 잠이 드는데 멜라토닌이 체온을 낮추는 역할을 하여 불면증 치료제로 쓰이기도 한다. 세로토닌은 햇빛이 있을 때 생성되는 행복 호르몬으로 충분한 햇빛을 통해 활성화된다.

57% 고2 09월 모의고사 지문/문제 변형

## 01

밑줄 친 all afterimages of the past이 다음 글에서 의미하는 바로 가장 적절한 것은?

Science can only tell us how the world appears to us, not how it is different from our observation of it, and therefore science seems to be a long way from *right now*. When you look into space, you are looking into an ancient past. Some of the stars are already long dead yet we still see them because of their traveling light. Suppose that we are on one of those stars located roughly sixty million light-years away. If we had a really powerful telescope pointed at the earth, we would see the dinosaurs walking around. The extreme end of the universe is probably so old that if we had that telescope, we might be able to see the beginning. In addition to faraway things, even the immediate objects around us are all afterimages of the past because there is still a time lag for the reflection of light to reach our eyes. It takes some time for every sensation our body feels to be carried to the brain.

① Science has made great breakthrough than ever before.
② The world has begun to investigate the past to predict the future.
③ Science that is considered to have advanced is in fact stuck in the past.
④ Efforts should be made to narrow the time gap between the past and the present.
⑤ What we are seeing is the things of the past, which is due to the delay of the light.

➕ 빅뱅(Big Bang) 이론
우주의 기원에 대한 이론으로 모든 것이 대폭발 후 팽창하고 있으며 빅뱅 이후에 시공간이 생겨나 지금의 우주가 되었다고 본다. '대폭발 우주론'이라고도 부른다. 초기 우주는 온도와 밀도가 매우 높은 '원시 불덩이'였으나 팽창하면서 점차 식었으며, 이때 만들어진 원소들이 현재 우주의 대부분을 차지한다고 본다.

New Words

| □ appear | ~처럼 보이다 | □ extreme end | 극단 | □ afterimage | 잔상 |
| □ observation | 관찰 | □ in addition to | ~이외에도 | □ time lag | 시간상의 지체 |
| □ roughly | 대략 | □ immediate | 가까운, 당면한 | □ reflection | 반사, 반영 |

44% 고2 06월 모의고사 변형

# 02

다음 글의 내용을 한 문장으로 요약하고자 한다. 빈칸 (A), (B)에 들어갈 말로 가장 적절한 것은?

The wife of American physiologist Hudson Hoagland became sick with a severe flu. Dr. Hoagland found out an interesting phenomenon that whenever he left his wife's room for a short while, she complained about him having been gone for a long time. In the interest of scientific investigation, he asked his wife to count to 60. She had to count for what she felt was one minute, while he kept a record of her temperature. His wife was unwilling to accept this, and he quickly picked up that the hotter she was, the faster she counted. When her temperature was 38 degrees Celsius, for instance, she counted to 60 in 45 seconds. Although it was an experiment with only one sample, after a few more experiments, the doctor thought that there might be a chance that some kind of 'internal clock' inside our brain runs faster as our fever goes up.

↓

The results of Dr. Hoagland's investigation showed that his wife felt ____(A)____ time had passed than actually had as her body temperature ____(B)____ .

| | (A) | (B) | | (A) | (B) |
|---|---|---|---|---|---|
| ① | more | …… increased | ② | more | …… decreased |
| ③ | less | …… retained | ④ | less | …… dwindled |
| ⑤ | less | …… changed | | | |

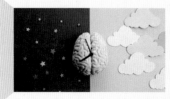

➕ 생체시계(circadian clock, biological clock)
생명체에 내재되어 있는 생물학적 시계로 일정한 리듬에 맞춰 움직이며 심장, 체온, 호흡, 수면, 배설, 혈압조절에 관여한다. 하지만 외부 요인에 의해 우선순위가 밀리기도 하는데, 인공조명으로 인해 음식을 먹는 시간대가 넓어져서 리듬이 깨져 주기 항상성이 흔들리기도 한다.

New Words

| ☐ physiologist | 생리학자 | ☐ phenomenon | 현상 | ☐ accept | 받아들이다 |
|---|---|---|---|---|---|
| ☐ severe | 심각한 | ☐ investigation | 탐구, 조사 | ☐ pick up | 알아채다 |
| ☐ flu | 독감 | ☐ unwilling | 마지못해 하는, 꺼리는 | ☐ internal | 내부의 |

# 03

**57%** 고2 09월 모의고사 지문/문제 변형

**다음 글의 내용을 한 문장으로 요약하고자 한다. 빈칸 (A), (B)에 들어갈 말로 가장 적절한 것은?**

There is no doubt that there is no story harsher than that of the Great Auk, the large black-and-white seabird found in northern oceans. Humans savagely destroyed their island populations until almost all of them were gone. Thanks to vicious and unpredictable ocean currents, there remained a special island that humankind couldn't reach, where the very last colony found safety. The currents there prevented humans from making any kind of safe landing. After enjoying a few years of comparative safety, a different kind of disaster happened to the Great Auk. Volcanic activity caused the island refuge to sink completely beneath the waves, and surviving individuals were forced to find shelter elsewhere. The new island home they chose lacked the benefits of the old in one terrible way. Humans could access it easily, and they did! Within just a few years this once-plentiful species was entirely extinct.

*savagely 잔혹하게

↓

| The Great Auk fled to an island ____(A)____ by humans, but the last few individuals were completely ____(B)____ by humans. |
| --- |

|  | (A) | (B) |  | (A) | (B) |
| --- | --- | --- | --- | --- | --- |
| ① | unknown | ...... fostered | ② | congested | ...... perished |
| ③ | abandoned | ...... retained | ④ | unreachable | ...... eliminated |
| ⑤ | underestimated | ...... changed |  |  |  |

**➕ 지구의 대멸종 시기**

종의 75% 이상이 한 번에 사라지는 것을 말하며, 지구에는 6500만 년 전 공룡의 멸종을 포함한 다섯 번의 대멸종 시기가 있었다. 다음 대멸종 시기는 화산, 지각운동, 운석 같은 지구 내부 문제가 아닌 인류에 의해 진행될 것이라고 과학자들은 경고한다.

| New Words | | | | | |
| --- | --- | --- | --- | --- | --- |
| ☐ population | 개체군 | ☐ volcanic | 화산의 | ☐ access | 접근하다; 접근 |
| ☐ vicious | 사나운, 거센 | ☐ refuge | 피난처 | ☐ once-plentiful | 한때 많았던 |
| ☐ ocean currents | 해류 | ☐ sink | 가라앉다 | ☐ extinct | 멸종된 |
| ☐ colony | 군락, 집단 | ☐ shelter | 피난(처) | ☐ flee | 도망가다 |

**01**  다음 주어진 단어를 활용하여 빈칸을 완성하시오.

intrinsic        last        in addition to        unwilling        vicious

(1)  The pain will _____ for five days.

(2)  He was attacked by a(n) _____ dog.

(3)  Many people say that gold doesn't have any _____ value.

(4)  They are _____ to invest more money in the project.

(5)  _____ the experience I have in this field, I also have the skills necessary for this job.

**02**  다음 영영풀이에 해당하는 단어를 보기에서 골라 쓰시오.

보기        colony        pick up        perish        observation        internal
access        regulation        matter        immediate        phenomenon

(1)  _____ : to be important

(2)  _____ : to approach or enter a place

(3)  _____ : to become aware of something

(4)  _____ : directly next to a particular place

(5)  _____ : existing or located on the inside of something

(6)  _____ : to disappear or be destroyed; to cease to exist

(7)  _____ : the controlling of an activity or process, usually by rules

(8)  _____ : a group of people with the same origin, occupation, interests, etc.

(9)  _____ : the act of careful watching and listening to someone or something

(10) _____ : an interesting fact or event that is difficult to understand or explain fully

# UNIT 06 스포츠, 취미, 여행

**주 제 소 개**  여가생활과 관련이 있는 분야로, 비교적 쉽게 접근할 수 있는 편이다. 스포츠의 역사나 관련 인물 또는 다양한 취미와 관련된 글이 제시되며, 환경보호 문제와 지속 가능한 환경 관광(sustainable eco-tourism) 등에 관한 내용을 다룬다. 대의파악(글의 주제, 제목, 요지) 및 내용 파악 유형으로 주로 출제된다.

---

**Q**  다음 글의 주제로 가장 적절한 것은?    76% 고1 03월 모의고사 변형

Collecting can open up new worlds for children. Collecting stamps, for example, shows them cultures or historical events of a country, such as national holidays and changes of government. ❶Plant or animal specimens, whether collected by children or not, can arouse their curiosity about the natural world. ❷Collecting also gives children opportunities to learn skills that can be used in their daily lives. One good example of these skills is that children can learn to organize their treasures by size, shape, or color while they are playing with collections such as dolls, comic books, stickers, and so on. This will help them to see the world from different points of view. When they think about the relationships among their pieces, they may realize that things in the world are connected with each other.

① how to start collecting
② why children like collecting
③ importance of leisure activities
④ where to keep your collections
⑤ educational effects of collecting

---

New Words

| | | | | | |
|---|---|---|---|---|---|
| ☐ collect | 수집하다 | ☐ skill | 기술 | ☐ and so on | 기타 등등 |
| ☐ government | 정부 | ☐ collection | 수집(품) | ☐ point of view | 관점 |
| ☐ specimen | 표본 | ☐ organize | 구성하다 | ☐ relationship | 관계 |
| ☐ arouse | 불러일으키다 | ☐ treasure | 보물 | ☐ piece | 조각, 작품 |
| ☐ curiosity | 호기심 | ☐ shape | 모양 | ☐ realize | 깨닫다, 실현하다 |
| ☐ opportunity | 기회 | ☐ comic book | 만화책 | ☐ be connected with | ~와 관련이 있다 |

## Reading Check

**빈칸에 들어갈 알맞은 말을 지문에서 찾아 적어 보세요.**

| 주제 | <sup>1</sup>_____ offers new opportunities for children |
|---|---|
| 예시 ① | • Collecting stamps teaches <sup>2</sup>_____ and <sup>3</sup>_____ events.<br>• Animal or plant <sup>4</sup>_____ teach us about the natural world. |
| 예시 ② | • Collecting provides opportunities to learn <sup>5</sup>_____ used in everyday life.<br>• Collecting helps see the world from a <sup>6</sup>_____ point of view by <sup>7</sup>_____ collections. |

## Analyzing Sentences

❶ Plant or animal specimens, [**whether** collected by children or not], can arouse their curiosity about the natural world.

⋯ [ ]는 양보의 부사절을 이끄는 부사절로 접속사 whether 다음에 '주어+be동사(they are)'가 생략되었다.

❷ Collecting also gives children **opportunities** [to learn skills] {that can be used in their daily lives}.

⋯ [ ]는 직접목적어인 opportunities를 수식하는 부정사의 형용사적 용법이며, { }는 선행사 skills를 수식하는 주격 관계대명사절이다.

**Background Knowledge**

**호모 콜렉투스(Homo Collectus)**
초기 인류들은 채집을 통해 생존 욕구 또는 주술적인 의미에서 동물 뼈 등을 수집했다. 현대에는 개인의 취미나 연구를 위해 특정한 물건이나 재료를 찾아 모은다. Maslow 가 수집하려는 욕구를 가장 기본적인 생리학적 범주에서 비롯된다고 보는 등, 수집은 인간의 한 특징적인 모습을 보여준다. 최근에는 수집을 전문으로 하는 사람들을 호모 콜렉투스, 즉 '수집하는 인간'이라고 부르는 신조어도 생겼다.

# 01

다음 글의 밑줄 친 부분 중, 어법상 틀린 것은?

49% 고1 09월 모의고사 변형

The city of Pompeii is a ① partially buried Roman town-city located near modern Naples in Italy. Pompeii, along with its surrounding area, was destroyed and buried ② during a long eruption of the volcano Mount Vesuvius in 79 AD. The eruption buried Pompeii under 4 to 6 meters of ash and stone, and it ③ lost for over 1,500 years before its accidental rediscovery in 1599. Since then, although much of the evidence of its inhabitants was lost in the excavations, its rediscovery still ④ has provided a detailed insight into life at the height of the Roman Empire. Today, Pompeii is a UNESCO World Heritage Site and is one of Italy's most popular tourist attractions, with approximately 2.5 million people ⑤ visiting every year.

✚ 헤라쿨라네움(Herculaneum)
오늘날 이탈리아 남부의 에르콜라노(Ercolano)지역에 있었던 고대 도시로 베수비우스 화산 분출 당시 폼페이와 함께 묻혔다. 현재 전체 면적의 4분의 1 정도가 발굴되었다. 상업도시의 특징이 많이 나타나는 폼페이에 비해 헤라쿨라네움은 그리스식 고급 주택단지로 추정된다. 폼페이와 함께 UNESCO 세계문화유산으로 지정되었다.

New Words

| | | | | | |
|---|---|---|---|---|---|
| □ partially | 부분적으로 | □ eruption | 분출 | □ excavation | 발굴 |
| □ bury | 묻다, 덮다 | □ volcano | 화산 | □ detailed | 상세한 |
| □ located | 위치한 | □ ash | (화산)재 | □ insight | 통찰력 |
| □ modern | 오늘날의, 현대의 | □ accidental | 우연한 | □ at the height of | ~의 전성기 때에 |
| □ along with | ~와 함께 | □ rediscovery | 재발견 | □ tourist attractions | 관광 명소 |
| □ destroy | 파괴하다 | □ inhabitant | 거주자 | □ approximately | 약, 대략 |

## 02 다음 글의 제목으로 가장 적절한 것은?

75% 고2 11월 모의고사 변형

We generally believe sport is a way of reducing violence. In a classic study, anthropologist Richard Sipes focuses on "combative sports," which, he says, include actual body contact between opponents, and hypothesizes that if sport is an alternative to violence, one would expect to find a negative correlation between the popularity of combative sports and the frequency and intensity of warfare. In other words, the more combative sports (e.g., football, boxing), the less likely warfare. Using a sample of 20 societies, Sipes tests the hypothesis and discovers a significant relationship between combative sports and violence. According to him, the more common and popular combative sports are in a society, the more likely that society is to engage in war. So, Sipes draws the obvious conclusion that combative sports are not alternatives to war but rather are reflections of the same aggressive impulses in human society.

① Is There a Distinction among Combative Sports?

② Combative Sports Mirror Human Aggressiveness

③ Never Let Your Aggressive Impulses Consume You!

④ International Conflicts: Creating New Military Alliances

⑤ Combative Sports Are More Common among the Oppressed

**➕ 전쟁과 스포츠의 연관성**
스포츠가 전쟁의 대안이라고 여겨지기도 하는데, 이는 스포츠가 폭력으로부터의 공격적인 경향을 전환시키는 안전밸브 역할을 할 수 있음을 말한다. 1970년대 미국 정부의 '핑퐁외교(Ping Pong Diplomacy)'는 탁구 경기를 통해 냉전시대 미국과 중국의 관계 개선을 이룬 사례이다.

**New Words**

| | | | | | |
|---|---|---|---|---|---|
| violence | 폭력 | alternative | 대체물 | hypothesis | 가설 |
| anthropologist | 인류학자 | negative | 부정적인 | significant | 중요한 |
| combative | 전투적인 | correlation | 상관관계 | engage in | ~에 참여하다 |
| contact | 접촉 | frequency | 빈도 | obvious | 명백한 |
| opponent | 상대방 | intensity | 강도 | aggressive | 공격적인 |
| hypothesize | 가설을 세우다 | warfare | 전투, 전쟁 | impulse | 충동 |

# 03 글의 흐름으로 보아, 주어진 문장이 들어가기에 가장 적절한 곳은?

40% 고3 06월 모의고사 변형

> There is a considerable difference as to whether people watch a film about the Himalayas on television and become excited by the 'untouched nature', or whether they go on a trek to Nepal.

Tourism takes place simultaneously in the realm of the imagination and that of the physical world. In contrast to literature or film, tourism leads to 'real', tangible worlds, while it nevertheless has the elements of fantasies, dreams, and myth, leading us to intangible worlds of mythological ideas. ( ① ) Even in the latter case, they remain, at least partly, in an imaginary world. ( ② ) They experience moments that they have already seen at home in books and films. ( ③ ) Their notions of untouched nature will probably be confirmed. ( ④ ) But now this confirmation is based on a physical experience. ( ⑤ ) The myth is thus experienced in a much more powerful way than by television, movies or books.

➕ 산티아고 순례길(Camino de Santiago)
1993년 UNESCO 세계문화유산으로 지정된 순례길로 예수의 열두제자였던 성 야고보의 무덤이 있는 산티아고 데 콤포스텔라(Santiago de Compostela)로 향하는 약 800km의 길이다. 성자(聖者)가 순교한 곳과 주변의 성지를 통해 종교적인 믿음을 더욱 강하게 하는 계기가 된다. 이슬람교인들이 메카순례를 하는 것과 동일한 의미라고 볼 수 있다.

**New Words**

| | | | | | |
|---|---|---|---|---|---|
| ☐ considerable | 상당한 | ☐ realm | 영역 | ☐ latter | 후자 |
| ☐ as to | ~에 관해 | ☐ physical | 물리적인 | ☐ at least | 적어도 |
| ☐ untouched | 손이 닿지 않은 | ☐ tangible | 유형의 | ☐ imaginary | 상상의, 가상의 |
| ☐ go on a trek | 긴 여행을 하다 | ☐ element | 요소 | ☐ confirm | 확실히 하다 |
| ☐ take place | 발생하다, 일어나다 | ☐ intangible | 무형의 | ☐ confirmation | 확고함 |
| ☐ simultaneously | 동시에 | ☐ mythological | 신화적인, 신화의 | ☐ be based on | ~에 기반[근거]을 두다 |

**01** 다음 주어진 단어를 활용하여 빈칸을 완성하시오.

| specimen | eruption | relationship | hypothesis | realm |

(1) There is often a lot of uncertainty in the _____ of science.

(2) There is no scientific evidence to support such a _____.

(3) Social interaction is always vulnerable to _____ of violence, greed, and selfishness.

(4) They found cooked grains and plants in the teeth of preserved Neanderthal _____.

(5) The case shows the role they play in determining the nature of the _____ between goods and services.

**02** 다음 영영풀이에 해당하는 단어를 보기에서 골라 쓰시오.

보기

| arouse | organize | bury | accidental | detailed |
| alternative | insight | combative | opponent | imaginary |

(1) _____ : including a lot of information

(2) _____ : to hide something in the ground

(3) _____ : to cause an emotional or mental state

(4) _____ : existing only in your mind or imagination

(5) _____ : having or showing a willingness to fight or argue

(6) _____ : happening in a way that is not planned or intended

(7) _____ : something that can be chosen instead of something else

(8) _____ : the ability to understand people and situations in a very clear way

(9) _____ : to arrange or order things so that they can be found or used easily

(10) _____ : a person, team, group, etc., that is competing against another in a contest

# 음악, 미술, 영화

**주제 소개**  예술과 관련된 주제 영역으로, 특정 시대의 예술 경향이나 역사, 발달 과정, 특정 예술인에 관한 글에 이르기까지 폭넓은 분야의 글이 다양하게 출제 된다. 예술사나 영화의 발달과정을 다루는 경우 글의 순서, 흐름에 무관한 문장 찾기 등의 유형으로 출제되지만, 대부분의 글은 연대순으로 진행되는 편이다.

**Q**  **다음 글의 주제로 가장 적절한 것은?**  75% 고1 11월 모의고사 변형

Sometimes, we are fascinated when our assumptions are turned inside out and around. The artist Pablo Picasso, for example, used Cubism as a way to help us see the world in a different light. When you look at his famous work *Three Musicians*, **❶**he used abstract forms to shape the performers in such an unexpected way that you think that nothing makes sense. However, when you look at the painting a second time, the figures in the artwork come together. Picasso's work challenges your assumptions about how space and objects are used. His artwork helps you see the world from different perspectives, and reminds you that shapes, objects, and colors can be used in alternative ways. **❷**By looking at the painting, you can get an intrinsic pleasure that you have never experienced before.

① abstract style formed by balancing reality with fantasy
② artists' guild organized by cooperating with cultural institutions
③ great challenges experienced by musicians in the modern world
④ emotional intelligence enhanced by appreciating Cubist artworks
⑤ inner pleasure driven by viewing the world from different angles

**New Words**

| | | | | | |
|---|---|---|---|---|---|
| ☐ fascinated | 매료된 | ☐ form | 형태 | ☐ challenge | 도전하다 |
| ☐ assumption | 전제, 가정 | ☐ shape | 형상화하다 | ☐ object | 사물 |
| ☐ inside out | 뒤집어 | ☐ unexpected | 예상치 못한 | ☐ remind | 상기시키다 |
| ☐ Cubism | 큐비즘, 입체파 | ☐ make sense | 이치에 맞다 | ☐ alternative | 다른, 대안적인 |
| ☐ light | 시각, 견해 | ☐ figure | 인물, 형태 | ☐ intrinsic | 내적인, 본질적인 |
| ☐ abstract | 추상적인 | ☐ artwork | (예술) 작품 | | |

**Reading Check**

빈칸에 들어갈 알맞은 말을 지문에서 찾아 적어 보세요.

| 도입<br>(주제문) | • We are fascinated when our assumptions are reversed. |
|---|---|
| 전개<br>(예시) | Pablo Picasso with ¹_____<br><br>• At first glance, the ²_____ form of the painting doesn't make sense.<br><br>• The second time, the ³_____ in the painting can be seen. |
| 발전<br>(부연) | • It makes us see the world from a different ⁴_____ by ⁵_____ our perceptions.<br><br>• It gives us intrinsic pleasure that we haven't ⁶_____ before. |

**Analyzing Sentences**

❶ ~, he used abstract forms to shape the performers in [**such** an unexpected way **that** you **think that** nothing makes sense].

···→ [ ]는 인과관계를 표현하는 such ~ that 구문으로 「such+a/an+형용사+명사」 다음에 결과의 부사절 접속사 that이 이끄는 문장이 이어진다. think 뒤의 접속사 that은 목적어 역할을 하는 명사절을 이끈다.

❷ **By looking at** the painting, you can get **an intrinsic pleasure** [**that** you have never experienced **before**].

···→ 「by+동사원형-ing」는 '~함으로써'라는 의미이고, [ ]는 앞에 있는 an intrinsic pleasure를 수식하는 주격 관계대명사절이다. before(~전에)는 단독으로 완료시제와 함께 쓰지만 ago는 과거시제에만 쓴다.

**Background Knowledge**

**입체파, 큐비즘(Cubism)**
피카소(Picasso)와 브라케(Braque)에 의해 창시된 20세기 유럽의 예술운동으로 르네상스 이후의 사실주의적 전통에서 해방시킨 회화 혁명으로 지칭된다. 과거의 회화가 '시각의 리얼리즘'이었다면 큐비즘은 '개념의 리얼리즘'을 주장하여 삼차원적인 현실세계의 개념을 이차원적 회화로 번역함과 동시에, 회화를 하나의 미적존재로 이루어내는 것을 목적으로 한다. Picasso가 그린 '아비뇽의 여인들'은 20세기 예술의 본질적인 기준점으로 인식된다.

66% 고1 09월 모의고사 변형

# 01

**다음 글의 내용을 한 문장으로 요약하고자 한다. 빈칸 (A), (B)에 들어갈 말로 가장 적절한 것은?**

Simply through a learned association, music could express emotion. Perhaps there is nothing inherently sad about a piece of music played in a minor key, or slowly with low notes. Maybe, the reason we have just come to hear certain kinds of music as sad is because we have learned to associate them in our culture with sad events like funerals. If this view is correct, we should have difficulty interpreting the emotions expressed in culturally unfamiliar music. In contrast, there is a view that finds resemblance in the link between music and emotion. For example, when we feel sad we move slowly and speak slowly and in a low-pitched voice. Thus when we hear slow, low music, we hear it as sad. If this view is correct, we should have little difficulty understanding the emotion expressed in culturally unfamiliar music.

↓

It is believed that emotion expressed in music can be understood through a(n) _____(A)_____ learned association or due to the _____(B)_____ between music and emotion.

| (A) | | (B) | | (A) | | (B) |
|---|---|---|---|---|---|---|
| ① culturally | …… | similarity | | ② culturally | …… | balance |
| ③ socially | …… | difference | | ④ incorrectly | …… | connection |
| ⑤ incorrectly | …… | contrast | | | | |

➕ **민족음악학(Ethnomusicology)**

민족문화의 맥락 속에서 음악을 이해하는 것으로 곡조, 박자, 소리의 특징과 표현법을 문화 요소와 결부시켜서 해석하여, 문화의 특질과 음악 간의 상관성을 밝혀내는 학문이다. Alan Lomax는 세계 각지에서 수집한 3,500곡의 민요 분석을 통해 문화마다의 고유한 음악적 특징을 확인하였다.

**New Words**

| | | | | | |
|---|---|---|---|---|---|
| □ association | 연상, 연관성 | □ associate | 연관시키다 | □ unfamiliar | 친숙하지 않은 |
| □ inherently | 본질적으로 | □ funeral | 장례식 | □ resemblance | 유사성 |
| □ minor key | 단조 | □ have difficulty -ing | ~하는데 어려움을 겪다 | □ link | 연결고리 |
| □ note | 음, 음조 | □ interpret | 해석하다 | □ low-pitched | 낮은 음역의 |

## 02

다음 글의 밑줄 친 부분 중, 문맥상 낱말의 쓰임이 적절하지 <u>않은</u> 것은?    53% 고2 03월 모의고사 변형

Theoretically, painters have an endless range of colors available for their use, especially in modern times with the chromatic ① <u>explosion</u> of synthetic chemistry. However, painters don't use all the colors at once, and indeed many of them have used a remarkably ② <u>restrictive</u> selection. Mondrian limited himself mostly to the three primary colors — red, yellow and blue — to fill his black-ruled grids, and Kasimir Malevich worked with similar self-imposed limits. For Yves Klein, one color was ③ <u>enough</u>. There was nothing ④ <u>new</u> in this because the Greeks and Romans also tended to use only red, yellow, black and white. Why? It's impossible to generalize, but both in antiquity and modernity it seems likely that the ⑤ <u>expanded</u> colors promoted clarity and comprehensibility, and helped to focus attention on the components that were important: shape and form.

*chromatic 유채색의 **grid 격자무늬

**➕ 피트 몬드리안(Piet Mondrian)**
네덜란드 출신의 근대 미술화가로 추상주의 회화의 거장이다. 몬드리안의 그림들은 강렬한 추상성이 특징으로 빨강, 파랑, 노랑인 삼원색의 직사각형 면과 무채색의 흰색, 검은색 면, 수직선, 수평선이 어우러져 있다. 이런 형태를 중요하게 다룬 추상화는 신조형주의가 추구한 양식의 두드러진 특징이 되었다.

New Words

| | | | | | |
|---|---|---|---|---|---|
| ☐ theoretically | 이론적으로 | ☐ indeed | 실제로 | ☐ generalize | 일반화하다 |
| ☐ endless | 무한한, 끝없는 | ☐ remarkably | 눈에 띄게 | ☐ modernity | 현대 |
| ☐ range | 범위 | ☐ restrictive | 제한적인 | ↔ antiquity | 고대 |
| ☐ available | 이용 가능한 | ☐ three primary colors | 삼원색 | ☐ promote | 촉진하다 |
| ☐ explosion | 폭발 | ☐ black-ruled | 검정색 선이 있는 | ☐ clarity | 명확성 |
| ☐ synthetic | 합성의 | ☐ self-imposed | 스스로 부과한 | ☐ component | 요소 |
| | | | | ☐ comprehensibility | 이해 가능성 |

# 03

글의 흐름으로 보아, 주어진 문장이 들어가기에 가장 적절한 곳은?    42% 고3 04월 모의고사 변형

> Under such circumstances, recycling previously composed music was the only way to make it more durable.

In the classical period of European music, people considered much musical material *de facto* common property. ( ① ) When Antonio Vivaldi performed in Venice his opera Rosmira fedele, the score not only had Vivaldi's own ideas but other composers'. ( ② ) As far as recycling of segments of music is concerned, we need to observe how today's composers are kept from doing so for many reasons. ( ③ ) A practical one is that each new piece is sure to remain available, in score or as an audio file. ( ④ ) In the 18th century, on the contrary, once the performing of a new piece was over, it became almost impossible to hear it again. ( ⑤ ) And if new pieces also contained ideas from other composers, that would reinforce European musical traditions by increasing the circulation of melodies and harmonic patterns people loved to hear.

*de facto 사실상 **segment 부분

**➕ 표절과 오마주**

표절(plagiarism)은 다른 사람의 저작물의 일부 또는 전부를 직접 베끼거나 모방하면서 자신의 독창적인 것처럼 밝히는 것을 말한다. 오마주(hommage)는 존경, 존중을 뜻하는 프랑스어인데, 존경하는 작가와 작품에 영향을 받아 비슷한 작품을 창작하거나 원작 그대로 표현하는 것을 말한다.

| New Words | | | | | |
|---|---|---|---|---|---|
| ☐ circumstances | 상황 | ☐ score | 악보 | ☐ practical | 실질적인 |
| ☐ recycle | 재활용하다 | ☐ composer | 작곡가 | ☐ be sure to 동사원형 | 틀림없이 ~하다 |
| ☐ previously | 이전에 | ☐ as far as ~ be concerned | ~에 관한 한 | ☐ contain | 포함하다 |
| ☐ durable | 오래가는 | | | ☐ reinforce | 강화하다 |
| ☐ material | 자료 | ☐ observe | 관찰하다 | ☐ circulation | 순환 |
| ☐ common property | 공유물 | ☐ keep ... from -ing | ...가 ~하는 것을 막다 | ☐ harmonic | 화성의 |

**01** 다음 주어진 단어를 활용하여 빈칸을 완성하시오.

explosion　　circulation　　score　　assumption　　associate

(1) Igor Stravinsky wrote the ＿＿＿＿＿＿＿ for his ballet Apollo Musagetes in six parts.

(2) The need for some ＿＿＿＿＿＿＿ of air is related to the control of moisture.

(3) If you use correct logic and valid ＿＿＿＿＿＿＿, then you will come to correct conclusions.

(4) The great ＿＿＿＿＿＿＿ of scientific creativity in Europe was helped by the spread of information.

(5) Learners ＿＿＿＿＿＿＿ new words with keywords that have similar sounds in their native language.

**02** 다음 영영풀이에 해당하는 단어를 보기에서 골라 쓰시오.

보기　　restrictive　　association　　durable　　component　　interpret
　　　　clarity　　abstract　　promote　　reinforce　　remind

(1) ＿＿＿＿＿＿＿ : to explain the meaning of something

(2) ＿＿＿＿＿＿＿ : limiting or controlling someone or something

(3) ＿＿＿＿＿＿＿ : to make someone think about something again

(4) ＿＿＿＿＿＿＿ : to help something happen, develop, or increase

(5) ＿＿＿＿＿＿＿ : one of the parts of something such as a system

(6) ＿＿＿＿＿＿＿ : staying strong and in good condition over a long period of time

(7) ＿＿＿＿＿＿＿ : to strengthen a group of people with new supplies or more people

(8) ＿＿＿＿＿＿＿ : the quality of being expressed, understood, etc., in an exact way

(9) ＿＿＿＿＿＿＿ : relating to general ideas rather than specific people, objects, etc.

(10) ＿＿＿＿＿＿＿ : a feeling, memory, or thought that is connected to a person, place, or thing

주 제 소 개   주로 작가의 예술작품을 소개하거나 유명한 건물 또는 장소에 관해 다루는 분야로 수능에서는 내용 파악, 글의 순서, 문장 삽입, 글의 제목, 빈칸 완성 유형 순으로 많이 출제되는 경향이 있다. 사실관계를 확인하며 객관적으로 글을 파악해야 한다.

**Q** 주어진 글 다음에 이어질 글의 순서로 가장 적절한 것을 고르시오.   70% 고2 09월 모의고사 지문/문제 변형

> **❶**It is impossible to imagine a modern city without glass. Meanwhile, we expect our buildings to protect us from the weather: this is what they are for, after all.

(A) The life we spend most of our time indoors is made light and delightful by glass. **❷**Glass windows have come to signify that we are open for business, and that the business will be honest and open. Namely, a shop without a shop window is essentially not a shop at all.

(B) The glass buildings rising every day in a modern city are the engineering answer to these conflicting desires: to be at once sheltered from various types of weather, to be secure from intrusion, but not to live in darkness.

(C) Nevertheless, faced with a prospective new home or place of work, one of the first questions people ask is: how much natural light is there?

① (A) – (C) – (B)   ② (B) – (A) – (C)   ③ (B) – (C) – (A)
④ (C) – (A) – (B)   ⑤ (C) – (B) – (A)

---

New Words

| | | | | | |
|---|---|---|---|---|---|
| □ protect | 보호하다 | □ essentially | 본질적으로 | □ shelter | 보호하다 |
| □ what ~ for | ~하는 이유 | □ rise | 솟아오르다, 떠오르다 | □ secure | 안전한 |
| □ delightful | 즐거운 | □ engineering | 공학적인 | □ intrusion | 침입 |
| □ signify | 의미하다 | □ conflicting | 상충하는 | □ prospective | 장래의, 유망한 |
| □ namely | 즉, 다시 말하면 | □ at once | 즉시, 동시에 | □ natural light | 자연광 |

## Reading Check

빈칸에 들어갈 알맞은 말을 지문에서 찾아 적어 보세요.

| 도입 | • It is impossible to think of a modern city without ¹_____. <br> • We expect our buildings to protect us from the weather. |
|---|---|
| 전개 <br> (예시) | • The glass buildings are the answer to ²_____ desires: <br>   – to be ³_____ from various types of weather, to be <br>    ⁴_____ from intrusion <br>   – but not to live in darkness |
| 발전 <br> (부연) | • The life is made ⁵_____ and ⁶_____ by glass. <br> • A shop without a ⁷_____ _____ is essentially not a shop at all. |

## Analyzing Sentences

❶ **It** is impossible **to imagine** a modern city without glass.

⋯➤ It은 형식상의 주어(가주어)로 해석되지 않으며 to부정사인 to imagine ~가 내용상의 주어(진주어)이다. 주어가 길어지면 그 자리에 가주어 It을 쓰고 진주어를 문장의 뒤로 보낸다.

❷ Glass windows have come to signify [**that** we are open for business], and [**that** the business will be honest and open].

⋯➤ [ ]는 signify의 목적어 역할을 하는 that절이며 and가 that절 두 개를 연결하는 병렬 구조이다. 병렬 구조에서 연결된 요소는 문법적으로 같은 형태여야 한다.

---

**Background Knowledge**

**건축 유리의 역사**

기원전 1세기경 로마에서 핸드 블로잉(Hand Blowing) 기법으로 투명한 유리가 만들어져서 가는 유리 조각을 틀에 끼워 창으로 사용하였다. 이후 긴 막대기 끝에 유리를 돌려 원형의 유리판을 만들고 끝을 잘라내어 사각형의 편평한 유리를 만들었다. 기술이 발전하면서 창유리는 점점 커졌고 실내는 더 밝아졌다. 유리의 대량생산이 가능해지면서 유리는 20세기 건축을 대표하는 재료가 되었다.

50% 고2 06월 모의고사 지문/문제 변형

## 01 다음 글의 밑줄 친 부분 중, 문맥상 낱말의 쓰임이 적절하지 <u>않은</u> 것은?

Our culture is biased towards the fine arts — those creative products which have no function other than pleasure. Craft objects are less ① <u>valuable</u>; because they serve an everyday function, they're not purely creative. But this division is culturally and historically ② <u>relative</u>. Most contemporary high art began as some kind of craft. The composition and performance of what we now call "classical music" began as a form of craft music ③ <u>ignoring</u> required functions in the Catholic mass, or the specific entertainment needs of royal patrons. For example, chamber music really was designed to be performed in chambers — small ④ <u>intimate</u> rooms in wealthy homes — often as background music. The dances that were composed by famous composers from Bach to Chopin indeed originally accompanied dancing. But today, with the contexts and functions for which they were composed ⑤ <u>gone</u>, we listen to these works as fine art.

\*mass 미사 \*\*patron 후원자

➕ **실내악(Chamber Music)의 유래**
실내악은 이탈리아어의 뮤지카 다 카메라(musica da camera)에서 유래된 말로, 귀족이나 왕후의 개인 공간, 부유한 대저택의 가정집에서 연주되는 음악을 말했다. 하지만 19세기에 들어와서 모든 예술음악이 연주 회장에서 연주를 하게 되면서 실내악은 소수 악기의 연주 형태를 가리키는 개념이 되었다.

| New Words | | | | | |
|---|---|---|---|---|---|
| ☐ biased | 편향된 | ☐ division | 구분 | ☐ royal | 왕실의 |
| ☐ fine art | 순수 예술 | ☐ relative | 상대적인 | ☐ chamber music | 실내악 |
| ☐ function | 기능 | ☐ contemporary | 현대의 | ☐ intimate | 친근한 |
| ☐ serve | 제공하다 | ☐ composition | 작곡 | ☐ accompany | 동반하다 |
| ☐ purely | 순전히, 전적으로 | ☐ specific | 구체적인 | ☐ context | 맥락, 상황 |

## 02 글의 흐름으로 보아, 주어진 문장이 들어가기에 가장 적절한 곳은?

49% 고2 11월 모의고사 변형

> It is possible to acquire more natural-looking portraits when the camera shoots from the same level as the child's eyeline in place of being tilted.

The birth of a child in a family is often the reason for which people begin to take up or rediscover photography. ( ① ) In many ways, photographing a child is little different from photographing any other person. ( ② ) All that makes it different, however, is the relative height between a young child and an adult. ( ③ ) Using the camera at your own head height works well for taking pictures of adults, but for children the camera will be tilted downward. ( ④ ) You look down on the child, literally and metaphorically, and the resulting picture can make the child look smaller and less important than most parents want. ( ⑤ ) For an eight year old, this might mean sitting down when shooting; and for a crawling baby, the best method may be to lie on the floor.

**➕ 카메라 앵글(Camera Angle)**
앵글은 대상(피사체)을 표현하고자 하는 카메라의 시점 또는 각도를 뜻한다. 위에서 아래로 대상을 내려다보는 시점을 하이앵글(high angle), 아래에서 위로 대상을 올려다보는 시점을 로우앵글(low angle)이라고 하는데, 대상을 주관적으로 표현하고 싶을 때 의도적으로 사용할 수 있다. 위에서 대상을 내려다보는 하이앵글은 대상을 좀 더 연약한 약자의 이미지로 만들어 낸다.

| New Words | | | | | |
|---|---|---|---|---|---|
| □ acquire | 얻다, 습득하다 | □ tilt | 기울다, 기울이다 | □ literally | 문자 그대로 |
| □ portrait | 인물 사진 | □ take up | ~을 배우다, 시작하다 | □ metaphorically | 비유적으로 |
| □ shoot | 찍다, 촬영하다 | □ photograph | ~의 사진을 찍다 | □ resulting | 결과로 생긴 |
| □ eyeline | 시선 | □ height | 신장, 높이 | □ crawling | 기어 다니는 |
| □ in place of | ~대신에 | □ work | 효과가 있다 | □ method | 방법 |

## 03

다음 빈칸에 들어갈 말로 가장 적절한 것은?  52% 수능 변형

Over a period of time the buildings that provided social, legal, religious, and other rituals evolved into forms that we subsequently have come _____. This is a two-way process; the building provides the physical environment and setting for a particular social ritual such as traveling by train or going to the theater, as well as the symbolic setting. The meaning of buildings evolves and is established by experience and we in turn read our experience into buildings. Buildings evoke an empathetic reaction in our minds through these projected experiences, and the intensity of these reactions is determined by our culture, our beliefs, and our expectations. They tell stories because their form and spatial organization give us hints about how they should be used. Their physical layout encourages some uses and restrains others; we do not go backstage in a theater if we are not specifically invited.

*empathetic 공감할 수 있는

① to identify and relate to a new architectural trend
② to recognize and associate with those buildings' function
③ to define and refine by reflecting cross-cultural interactions
④ to use and change into an integral part of our environment
⑤ to alter and develop for the elimination of their meanings

➕ 스테인드 글라스(Stained glass)
색깔이 있는 유리, 착색된 유리라는 뜻으로 중세 유럽의 고딕 건축 양식과 함께 큰 발전을 이루었다. 고딕 성당의 스테인드 글라스는 성경 속 세상을 현실에 구현하고자 했으며, 실제로 어두운 실내에 스테인드 글라스를 통해 들어오는 빛은 신비하고 아름다운 효과를 연출한다.

New Words

| □ legal | 법적인 | □ symbolic | 상징적인 | □ intensity | 강도, 강함 |
| □ religious | 종교적인 | □ establish | 확립[설립]하다 | □ spatial | 공간의 |
| □ ritual | 의식 | □ in turn | 차례로, 결국 | □ layout | 배치 |
| □ evolve | 발전하다, 진화하다 | □ evoke | 불러일으키다 | □ restrain | 억제하다 |
| □ subsequently | 나중에 | □ reaction | 반응 | □ identify | 확인하다, 식별하다 |
| □ setting | 장소, 환경 | □ projected | 투사된, 투영된 | □ refine | 정제하다, 다듬다 |

**01** 다음 주어진 단어를 활용하여 빈칸을 완성하시오.

| signify | function | intimate | acquire | reaction |
|---|---|---|---|---|

(1) The news was shocking, but her _____ was very calm.

(2) This international peace treaty _____ the end of the war.

(3) The calculator has the critical _____ of solving math problems.

(4) Because of my driver's license, I could _____ the reputation as the best driver.

(5) It is necessary to have an _____ relationship between the employer and the employees.

**02** 다음 영영풀이에 해당하는 단어를 보기에서 골라 쓰시오.

| 보기 | secure | prospective | relative | contemporary | accompany |
|---|---|---|---|---|---|
| | tilt | method | evoke | intensity | restrain |

(1) _____ : to provoke or bring about

(2) _____ : belonging to the present time

(3) _____ : likely to happen at a future date

(4) _____ : to regulate or keep under control

(5) _____ : certain to remain safe and unthreatened

(6) _____ : to move or cause to move into a sloping position

(7) _____ : the measurable amount, force or strength of a property

(8) _____ : considered in relation or in proportion to something else

(9) _____ : to go somewhere with someone as a companion or escort

(10) _____ : a particular procedure for accomplishing or approaching something

# 교육, 학교, 진로

주로 교육이 지향하는 방향이나 학습에 영향을 끼치는 요소, 교육 방식의 문제점이나 개선 방안 등을 다루는 분야로 수능에서는 글의 요약, 내용 파악, 어법, 어휘 유형으로 가장 많이 출제되는 경향이 있지만 글의 주제, 제목, 그리고 빈칸 완성 유형으로도 출제되니 교육과 관련된 다양한 내용을 파악해야 한다.

**Q** 다음 글의 제목으로 가장 적절한 것은?   53% 고2 09월 모의고사 변형

At Naperville High School the students who struggle with math and reading go to gym class first. ❶"What we're trying to do here is jump start their brains," says Paul, the PE teacher. Physical education is the very first class of the day. Scientists say exercise is a perfect brain-builder; complicated movement stimulates thinking. Dr. Charles Hillman's research shows that after a 30-minute session on the treadmill, students actually do up to 10 percent better at problem solving. "Exercise is good for attention, information processing, and performance of cognitive tasks," says Hillman. Reading scores almost doubled in Naperville. Math scores are up by 20 percent. ❷In an era in which many schools are cutting PE programs so that they can save money, Naperville is looking for new activities to get kids moving.

① The Right Age to Start Group Exercise
② How Physical Education Transformed a School
③ Why Reading and Math Matter for Cognitive Skills
④ School Fundraising as an Investment for the Future
⑤ The Relationship between Brain Power and Athletic Ability

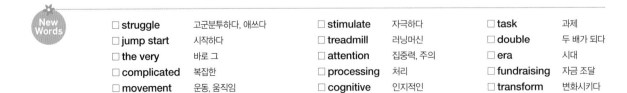

New Words

| | | | | | |
|---|---|---|---|---|---|
| □ struggle | 고군분투하다, 애쓰다 | □ stimulate | 자극하다 | □ task | 과제 |
| □ jump start | 시작하다 | □ treadmill | 러닝머신 | □ double | 두 배가 되다 |
| □ the very | 바로 그 | □ attention | 집중력, 주의 | □ era | 시대 |
| □ complicated | 복잡한 | □ processing | 처리 | □ fundraising | 자금 조달 |
| □ movement | 운동, 움직임 | □ cognitive | 인지적인 | □ transform | 변화시키다 |

 Reading Check

빈칸에 들어갈 알맞은 말을 지문에서 찾아 적어 보세요.

| 도입 | • The students who ¹_____ with math and reading go to gym class first. |
|---|---|
| 전개 | • Exercise is a ²_____ brain-builder.<br>– Complicated movement ³_____ thinking.<br>→ After a 30-minute treadmill workout, students do better at<br> ⁴_____ _____. |
| 발전<br>(결과) | • Unlike many schools, Naperville is looking for new ⁵_____ to get kids ⁶_____. |

Analyzing Sentences

❶ [**What** we're trying to do here] is [**jump start** their brains.]

⋯→ 첫 번째 [ ]는 선행사를 포함한 what이 이끄는 명사절로 문장의 주어이며, 두 번째 [ ]는 주격 보어 역할을 하는 to 부정사구로 jump start 앞에 to가 생략되어 있다.

❷ In an era [**in which** many schools are cutting PE programs {**so that** they can save money}], Naperville is looking for new activities to get kids moving.

⋯→ [ ]는 an era를 수식하는 관계절이고 그 안의 { }는 many schools are cutting PE programs의 목적을 설명하기 위해 쓰였다.

**Background Knowledge**

**운동과 학습 간의 관계**

아인슈타인의 뇌가 일반인과 다른 점은 좌뇌와 우뇌를 이어주는 '뇌량'이 특히 발달되어 있는 것으로 밝혀졌다. 똑똑한 뇌를 만들기 위해서는 뇌세포를 건강하게 하고 뇌량을 강화시켜야하는데 현대 뇌과학자들은 그것의 핵심이 바로 운동이라고 한다. 운동은 더 많은 산소와 혈액을 뇌에 공급해주며 새로운 뇌세포를 만드는 원료인 뇌성장단백질(BDNF)을 생성한다.

# 01

다음 글의 빈칸에 들어갈 말로 가장 적절한 것은?  89% 고2 11월 모의고사 변형

　　In general, students can experience a variety of activities at school. They join clubs and take part in school activities for a number of very good reasons. They have interests that they wish to pursue and skills that they wish to develop. From time to time, especially in high schools, students participate in extracurricular activities because it looks good on a college application or résumé. But the underlying reason for joining just about all school activities is to _____. Meeting new people who might be different from you is fun, and it's easy if you share an interest. It can be especially exciting to make friends with people who are not in your immediate social circle. By doing so, people can form a wide range of personal relationships and go through many different fields.

① prepare for a job
② change one's old habits
③ have a good body shape
④ make connections with others
⑤ broaden academic experiences

❖ 고등학교의 동아리 활동
학생들의 개성과 소질을 개발하고 지원하여 자연스러운 인간관계를 형성하여 창의력과 성취감, 자율성을 높이는데 목적이 있다. 특히 미국은 동아리 활동을 장려하고 있는데 예체능(음악, 미술, 체육 등) 분야에서 학생들의 참여가 활발하다.

New Words

| | | | | | |
|---|---|---|---|---|---|
| □ in general | 일반적으로 | □ participate in | 참가하다 | □ immediate | 가까운, 즉각적인 |
| □ take part in | 참가하다 | □ extracurricular | 과외의 | □ circle | 집단 |
| □ a number of | 많은 | □ application | 지원(서) | □ form | 형성하다 |
| □ pursue | 추구하다 | □ résumé | 이력서 | □ a wide range of | 폭넓은 |
| □ from time to time | 때때로 | □ underlying | 근본적인 | □ go through | 경험하다, 겪다 |
| □ especially | 특히 | □ share | 나누다 | □ broaden | 넓히다 |

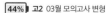

## 02

글의 흐름으로 보아, 주어진 문장이 들어가기에 가장 적절한 곳은? 44% 고2 03월 모의고사 변형

> I once worked with a group of students in the final year of senior school, and they listened out for the slang used in their school.

Slang is actually quite difficult for linguists to find out about. You will have your local slang you use in your school or in your town, and there's no way I would ever know about it if you did not tell me what it was. ( ① ) In fact, in your area you'll probably have several different sorts of slang. ( ② ) The slang kids use in primary school could possibly be different from that which is used in secondary school. ( ③ ) If your town has several schools, there are often differences in the kind of slang which is heard in each school. ( ④ ) Besides, there may even be words used differently within a single school. ( ⑤ ) They found that the slang which was used by first-year students was very different from their own.

➕ 은어 vs. 전문용어
은어는 어떤 계층이나 부류의 사람들이 다른 사람들이 알아듣지 못하도록 서로 빈번하게 사용하는 말로, 심마니(산삼을 캐는 사람들)끼리 통하는 말, 젊은 사람들끼리만 통하는 단어 등이 있다. 전문용어는 특정 학문이나 전문 분야에서 특별한 의미로 쓰는 말로 영어로는 terminology, jargon으로 칭한다.

New Words

| □ senior school | (영국의) 고등학교 | □ area | 지역, 구역 | □ difference | 차이(점) |
| □ slang | 은어, 속어 | □ several | 몇몇의, 몇 가지 | □ each | 각각의 |
| □ linguist | 언어학자 | □ sort of | 종류의 (= kind of) | □ besides | 게다가 |
| □ find out (about) | 파악하다, 알아내다 | □ primary school | 초등학교 | □ single | 단 하나의, 단일의 |
| □ local | 지역의, 현지의 | □ secondary school | 중등학교, 중학교 | □ own | 자신의 것; 자신의 |

정답과 해설 P.18

## 03 다음 글에서 글쓴이가 주장하는 바로 가장 적절한 것은?

[93%] 수능 변형

At the 2015 Fortune Most Powerful Women Summit, Ginni Rometty offered this advice: "When did you ever learn the most in your life? What experience? I am sure that you'll tell me it was a time that you felt at risk." In order to become a better leader, you have to get out of your comfort zone and become independent. You have to challenge the conventional ways of doing things and search for opportunities to innovate. Exercising leadership both expects you to challenge the organizational status quo and requires you to challenge your internal status quo. You have to venture beyond the boundaries of your current experience and explore new territory. Those are the places in which there are opportunities to improve, innovate, experiment, and grow. Growth is always at the edges, just outside the boundaries of where you are right now.

*status quo 현재 상태

① 지도자는 실현 가능한 목표를 설정해야 한다.
② 지도자는 새로운 제도를 적극적으로 도입해야 한다.
③ 지도자는 조직의 현재 상태를 철저히 분석해야 한다.
④ 지도자는 현재의 자신을 넘어서는 도전을 해야 한다.
⑤ 지도자는 기존의 방식과 새로운 방식을 조화시켜야 한다.

### ➕ 가장 영향력 있는 여성기업인 선정
미국 경제 잡지 중에 하나인 포춘(Fortune)지는 매년 전문가들로 구성된 위원회를 통해 영향력 있는 여성기업인을 2014년부터 선정해 발표하고 있다. 대륙별로(미주, 아시아—태평양, 유럽—중동—아프리카 지역) 나눠 선정하고, 사업 규모뿐 아니라 사회·문화적 영향력도 다각적으로 분석한다.

| | | | | | |
|---|---|---|---|---|---|
| ☐ summit | 회담 | ☐ conventional | 전통적인, 관례적인 | ☐ internal | 내적인, 내부의 |
| ☐ advice | 충고 | ☐ opportunity | 기회 | ☐ venture | 위험을 무릅쓰다 |
| ☐ be sure | 확신하다 | ☐ innovate | 혁신시키다 | ☐ boundary | 경계(선) |
| ☐ feel at risk | 위험을 느끼다 | ☐ challenge | 도전하다, 이의를 제기하다 | ☐ current | 현재의 |
| ☐ comfort zone | 안전지대 | ☐ organizational | 조직의, 단체의 | ☐ territory | 영역, 영토 |
| ☐ independent | 독립적인 | ☐ require | 요구하다 | ☐ edge | 가장자리, 모서리 |

**01** 다음 주어진 단어를 활용하여 빈칸을 완성하시오.

stimulate     immediate     slang     summit     venture

(1) We watched the inter-Korean _____ on TV.

(2) He does _____ investments in the field of bitcoin.

(3) When people learn a foreign language, they usually learn _____ first.

(4) The more _____ feedback we have, the more successful we can be.

(5) I used negative words to my student in order to _____ the emotions.


**02** 다음 영영풀이에 해당하는 단어를 보기에서 골라 쓰시오.

보기     struggle     cognitive     era     pursue     form
broaden     local     single     innovate     organizational

(1) _____ : only one; not one of several

(2) _____ : to strive in pursuit of a goal

(3) _____ : to do or introduce something new

(4) _____ : to go in search of, especially on the trail of

(5) _____ : relating to one's mental functions or abilities

(6) _____ : to make or be made into a specific shape or form

(7) _____ : being, or related to, a corporation, company or business

(8) _____ : to expand or increase to encompass more people or things

(9) _____ : relating or restricted to a particular area or one's neighborhood

(10) _____ : a time period of indeterminate length in history that is known for a particular event

# UNIT 10 언어, 문학

주 제 소 개  문학 작품 속 구체적인 장면을 다루기도 하지만, 특정 작가와 관련된 내용이나 문학에 관한 일반적인 정의, 작품이 독자에게 미치는 영향 등 문학의 사회적 기능과 역할에 관한 글이 자주 등장한다. 언어와 관련된 주제의 경우, 인간의 고유한 특징으로서의 언어에 관한 글이 자주 인용된다. 언어 간 특징이나 글쓰기, 음운학, 음성학 등 언어 이론에 관한 글도 간혹 출제된다.

**Q** 주어진 글 다음에 이어질 글의 순서로 가장 적절한 것은?　46% 고1 11월 모의고사 변형

> Literary works, in essence, suggest rather than explain; they imply rather than talk about their claims clearly and directly.

(A) What a text implies often gives us great interest. And our work of figuring out a text's implications tests our analytical powers. In considering what a text suggests, we gain practice in making sense of texts.

(B) But regardless of the proportion of its showing to telling, ❶there always remains something for readers to interpret. Thus we should ask what the text suggests as a way to approach literary interpretation, and as a way to begin thinking about its implications.

(C) This broad generalization, however, doesn't mean that literary works exclude direct statements. ❷Depending on when and by whom they were written, literary works may contain larger amounts of direct telling than those of suggestion and implication.

① (A) – (C) – (B)　② (B) – (A) – (C)　③ (B) – (C) – (A)
④ (C) – (A) – (B)　⑤ (C) – (B) – (A)

New Words

| □ literary | 문학의 | □ figure out | 알아내다 | □ generalization | 일반화 |
| □ in essence | 본질적으로 | □ analytical | 분석적인 | □ exclude | 배제하다 |
| □ suggest | 암시하다 | □ regardless of | ~와 관계없이 | □ statement | 진술 |
| □ imply | 함축하다 | □ proportion | 비율 | □ contain | 포함하다 |
| □ claim | 주장; 주장하다 | □ interpret | 해석하다 | □ implication | 함축 |
| □ directly | 직접적으로 | □ approach | ~에 접근하다 | □ make sense of | ~을 이해하다 |

## Reading Check

빈칸에 들어갈 알맞은 말을 지문에서 찾아 적어 보세요.

| 도입 | • Narrative style in literary works<br>– Literary works ¹＿＿＿＿＿＿＿ and imply rather than give<br>²＿＿＿＿＿＿＿ about the subject. |
|------|------|
| 전개 | • Depending on the time and author, there can be more direct<br>³＿＿＿＿＿＿＿ than ⁴＿＿＿＿＿＿＿.<br>• Readers must ⁵＿＿＿＿＿＿＿ what the literary work implies. |
| 발전 | • Discovering the implications of a text requires readers' ⁶＿＿＿＿＿＿＿ ability.<br>• When considering what the text implies, readers can understand a literary work. |

## Analyzing Sentences

❶ ~, there always remains something [**for readers**] **to interpret**.
⋯ there remains ~ 는 '~가 남아있다'의 뜻으로 뒤의 something이 문장의 주어이다.
to interpret은 something을 수식하는 부정사의 형용사적 용법으로 쓰였으며 [ ]는 to부정사의
의미상 주어이다.

❷ Depending on [**when and by whom** they were written], literary works may contain
{**larger amounts** of direct telling **than those** of suggestion and implication}.
⋯ [ ]는 전치사의 목적어로 쓴 간접의문문으로, 의문사 when과 by whom이 병렬 구조로
연결되어 있다. { }는 비교급 구문으로 those는 amounts를 가리킨다.

---

**Background Knowledge**

**말하기(telling)와 보여주기(showing)**

소크라테스가 제시한 대화 방식 중 하나인 디에게시스(Diegesis)는 사건이나 대화를 직접 보여주는 '보여주기'에 해당하는 것으로 화자는 사라지고 독자가 직접 결론을 이끌어 내야 한다. 이에 반해 미메시스(Mimesis)는 화자가 직접 이야기를 하고 요약하여 독자에게 설명하는 것으로 '말하기'에 해당한다. 소설에서 인물을 설정하고 성격을 묘사하는 방식인 직접제시는 '말하기'에 해당하고, 간접제시는 '보여주기'에 해당한다.

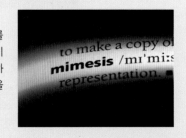

# 01 다음 빈칸에 들어갈 말로 가장 적절한 것은?

67% | 고1 09월 모의고사 변형

Many evolutionary biologists argue that humans _____. From ancient primitive societies, we needed to trade, and we needed to establish trust in order to trade. Language is very convenient when you are trying to conduct business with someone. Two early humans could not only agree to trade three wooden bowls for six bunches of bananas, but establish rules as well. What wood was used for the bowls? Where did you get the bananas? That business deal would have been nearly impossible using only gestures and confusing noises, and carrying it out according to terms which were agreed upon created a bond of trust. If so, how could they come to an agreement? Language. Language allows us to reach a consensus by expressing the specific, and this is where conversation plays a key role.

① used body language to communicate
② instinctively knew who to depend on
③ often changed rules for their own needs
④ lived independently for their own survival
⑤ developed language for economic reasons

**➕ 유전자 FOXP2**
FOXP2는 인간의 언어 구사에 중요한 역할을 하는 유전자로 2002년 영국의 연구팀이 발견하였다. 독일의 막스 플랑크 연구소는 20만 년 전부터 FOXP2 유전자에 변이가 일어나서 인간만이 정교한 음성언어를 구사할 수 있다고 보았다. 이는 포유동물이 모두 비슷한 유전자를 가졌지만, 언어구사능력이 유전자 일부 변이 때문이라는 사실을 밝힌 최초의 연구이다.

New Words

| □ evolutionary | 진화의 | □ convenient | 편리한 | □ terms | 조건 |
| □ economic | 경제적인 | □ conduct | (특정 활동을) 하다 | □ bond | 결속 |
| □ primitive | 원시적인 | □ bunch | 다발 | □ agreement | 합의, 동의 |
| □ trade | 거래하다 | □ deal | 거래 | □ consensus | 합의, 일치 |
| □ establish | 확립하다 | □ carry out | 실행하다 | □ specific | 구체적인 |

## 02 글의 흐름으로 보아, 주어진 문장이 들어가기에 가장 적절한 곳은?

66% 고2 09월 모의고사 변형

> But there's a difference between being well-read and knowing how to read well.

Critical reading is a way of reading that will enable you to look at literature in great depth and different perspectives. ( ① ) It's not an inborn but a learned skill that you will develop with some knowledge and experience. ( ② ) You may have heard certain people referred to as being well-read, which implies that they have read many different books and other forms of literature. ( ③ ) It means that it's not quantity but quality that matters. ( ④ ) To read critically means to read analytically, which requires that you question and think about the written material in front of you. ( ⑤ ) When you question something, it usually leads you to find answers, and these answers will give you insight into the author's intentions.

**➕ 비판적 읽기(Critical Reading)**
글의 내용을 이해하는 수준이 아니라, 작가의 주장이 옳은지, 논증 방식이 타당하고 논리적인지, 제시된 자료가 적절한지를 독자가 직접 따져가면서 글을 읽는 것을 말한다. 비판적 읽기는 객관적 증거에 비추어 상황을 비교, 검토하고 인과관계를 명백히 하는 비판적 사고에 기반을 둔 독서 행위로 오래전부터 강조되어 온 방식이며, 지식 기반의 사회로 변하는 과정에서 중요성이 강조되고 있다.

 New Words

| | | | | | |
|---|---|---|---|---|---|
| ☐ well-read | 많이 읽는, 다독의 | ☐ knowledge | 지식 | ☐ matter | 중요하다 |
| ☐ critical | 비판적인 | ☐ refer to A as B | A를 B라 언급하다 | ☐ analytically | 분석적으로 |
| ☐ in great depth | 대단히 깊이 | ☐ form | 형식 | ☐ in front of | ~앞에 |
| ☐ perspective | 관점, 시각 | ☐ quantity | 양 | ☐ insight | 통찰력 |
| ☐ inborn | 타고난 | ☐ quality | 질 | ☐ intention | 의도 |

# 03

다음 빈칸에 들어갈 말로 가장 적절한 것은?

While it is correct to say that we express and represent our thoughts in language, it may be a big mistake to suppose there are structural similarities between what is representing and what is represented. Robert Stalnaker suggests an analogy with the representation of *numbers*: The number 9 can be represented as '12 — 3' but it doesn't say that 12, 3, or subtraction are constituents of the number 9. Similarly, a thought might get expressed verbally with a particular linguistic structure. However, it doesn't mean that _____. Suppose, for example, that I look at a fruit bowl, and think that there is an apple and an orange in that bowl. What I see includes some pieces of fruit and a bowl, but there exists no object corresponding to the word 'and' either in the world or in my visual image.

*subtraction 빼기

① the thought itself has such a structure
② linguistic analysis of a thought is unlikely
③ the language in mind lacks a logical structure
④ a thought and its verbal expression are distinct
⑤ the sentence structurally differs from the thought

**➕ 시니피앙(Signifiant)과 시니피에(Sigfnifié)**
스위스의 언어학자인 소쉬르는 개념과 연합된 음성 형식(기호)을 시니피앙(Signifiant), 음성과 연합된 의미(내용)을 시니피에(Sigfnifié)라고 정의하면서, 언어를 구성하는 기호와 의미인 둘 사이에는 아무런 필연적인 관계가 없다는 언어 기호의 자의성을 설명했다.

New Words

| □ represent | 나타내다 | □ constituent | 구성요소 | □ include | 포함하다 |
|---|---|---|---|---|---|
| □ suppose | 가정하다 | □ verbally | 말로, 구두로 | □ exist | 존재하다 |
| □ structural | 구조적인 | □ particular | 특정한 | □ corresponding to | ~에 상응하는 |
| □ similarity | 유사성 | □ linguistic | 언어적인 | □ visual | 시각적인 |
| □ analogy | 비유 | □ structure | 구조 | | |

**01** 다음 주어진 단어를 활용하여 빈칸을 완성하시오.

proportion    statement    consensus    insight    bond

(1) Scientific _____ or remarks, even when they are valid, are not literature.

(2) When Rasputin showed that he was able to heal her son, their _____ became truly stronger.

(3) Paul kept a notebook of his artistic _____ and ideas and published a number of books.

(4) The assumption is that disagreement is wrong and _____ is the desirable state of things.

(5) Modern anthropologists report that gathering food only accounts for a small _____ of their time.

**02** 다음 영영풀이에 해당하는 단어를 보기에서 골라 쓰시오.

보기    generalization    interpret    primitive    analytical    convenient
inborn    analogy    constituent    linguistic    exclude

(1) _____ : relating to language

(2) _____ : to explain the meaning of something

(3) _____ : one of the parts that form something

(4) _____ : existing from the time someone is born

(5) _____ : to leave out something: to not include

(6) _____ : relating to the careful study of something

(7) _____ : belonging to an early or very ancient time

(8) _____ : allowing you to do something easily, without trouble

(9) _____ : a comparison of two things based on being alike in some way

(10) _____ : the act or process of forming opinions based on information

# 11 정보, 미디어

주 제 소 개  전 세계적으로 빠르게 변하고 있는 환경 속에서, 우리는 과거와 현재의 다양한 정보를 해석하고 활용한다. 정보를 주로 제공하는 대중매체(미디어)의 역할과 그것이 올바르게 나아갈 방향을 비판적인 시각으로 판단하도록 도움을 주는 내용이 자주 언급된다. 수능에서는 글의 제목, 주제, 빈칸 완성 등의 유형으로 주로 출제된다.

**Q** 다음 빈칸에 들어갈 말로 가장 적절한 것은?    67% 고2 03월 모의고사 변형

In 1944, the German rocket-bomb attacks on London suddenly escalated. Over two thousand V-1 flying bombs fell on the city, killing more than five thousand people and wounding many more. However, the Germans consistently missed their targets. ❶Bombs intended for Tower Bridge or Piccadilly fell well short of the city, landing in the less populated suburbs. ❷This was because, in fixing their targets, the Germans relied on secret agents they had planted in England. They did not know that these agents had been discovered by England and that English-controlled agents were giving them subtly deceptive information. The bombs would hit farther and farther from their targets whenever they fell. By the end of the attacks they were landing on cows in the country. By _____, the English army gained a strong advantage.

① being honest with the public

② giving the enemy a chance to retreat

③ feeding the enemy wrong information

④ focusing on one goal consistently

⑤ exploring the unknown places

**New Words**

| | | | | | |
|---|---|---|---|---|---|
| □ attack | 공격; 공격하다 | □ fall short of | ~에 못 미치다 | □ subtly | 교묘히, 묘하게 |
| □ escalate | 증가하다 | □ populated | 인구가 있는 | □ deceptive | 잘못된, 속이는 |
| □ wound | 부상을 입히다 | □ suburb | 교외 | □ whenever | ~할 때마다 |
| □ consistently | 지속적으로 | □ fix | 정하다, 고정시키다 | □ gain | 얻다 |
| □ target | 목표(물) | □ rely on | ~에 의지하다 | □ public | 대중; 공공의 |
| □ intended | 의도된 | □ secret agent | 비밀 요원 | □ retreat | 물러나다; 후퇴 |

## Reading Check

빈칸에 들어갈 알맞은 말을 지문에서 찾아 적어 보세요.

| 제목 | The effect of presenting ¹_____ on the situation of war |
|------|------|
| 진행 과정 | 1. Many flying bombs started to ²_____ on the city of London, England.<br><br>2. The bombs ³_____ to hit farther and farther away from London.<br><br>3. The England government hired ⁴_____ _____ to give the Germans ⁵_____ _____ about their targets. |

## Analyzing Sentences

❶ Bombs [**intended** for Tower Bridge or Piccadilly] fell well short of the city, landing in the less populated suburbs.

⋯ [ ] 부분은 과거분사 intended(의도된)로 이루어진 수식구로 문장의 주어 Bombs를 꾸며주고 있다.

❷ This was because, [**in fixing their targets**], the Germans relied on **secret agents** {they **had planted** in England}.

⋯ This was because 절 사이에 [ ] 부분인 「전치사 in + 동명사구(~할 때에)」가 삽입되었고, 선행사가 secret agents인 목적격 관계대명사가 생략된 절인 { } 부분에는 대과거를 나타내는 과거완료 had planted((이미) 심어놓았던)가 사용되었다.

**Background Knowledge**

**런던 대공습(The Blitz)**
제2차 세계 대전에서 독일 공군이 영국의 수도인 런던을 폭격한 대공습을 말한다. 히틀러의 독일군은 영국 왕립 공군을 궤멸시키고, 영국에 상륙을 시도했지만 수포로 돌아갔다. 영국이 베를린을 보복 폭격하자 히틀러와 괴링은 민간에 대한 폭격으로 전술을 바꾸었다. 1940년 9월 7일에서 1941년 5월 21일까지 런던을 비롯한 영국의 도시들은 총 100회 이상의 공습을 당했으며, 이 공습으로 약 45,000명이 영국인이 희생되었다.

# 01

**다음 빈칸에 들어갈 말로 가장 적절한 것은?**  48% 고2 09월 모의고사 변형

For many centuries European science and general knowledge were recorded in Latin. Latin was a language that no one spoke any longer at that time, so it had to be learned in schools. Very few individuals had the opportunity to study Latin. Even fewer could read books in that language or participate in the intellectual discourse of those times. Moreover, few people had access to books, which were handwritten, scarce, and expensive. However, the great explosion of scientific creativity in Europe helped spread information. Gutenberg invented movable type in printing, which led to the acceptance of everyday languages. And then, they rapidly replaced Latin as the medium of discourse. In sixteenth-century Europe it became much easier to make a creative contribution. Consequently, social supports became more favorable; _____.

*discourse 담화, 담론

① the number of rich people increased
② people were able to learn Latin more easily
③ information became more widely accessible
④ education provided equal opportunities for all
⑤ new methods of scientific research were introduced

**➕ 구텐베르크 & 고려의 인쇄술**
화약, 나침반, 종이와 함께 세계 4대 발명품 중 하나는 인쇄술로 독일의 구텐베르크가 활자를 발명하면서 유럽의 종교개혁과 산업혁명을 빠르게 발전시켰다. 한편, 세계가 공식적으로 인정하고 있는 가장 오래된 금속활자는 고려시대의 '직지심체요절'로 1377년 7월에 찍어낸 걸로 추정되는데, 구텐베르크보다 78년 이상 앞선 것이다.

New Words

| | | | | | |
|---|---|---|---|---|---|
| □ few | (극)소수의 | □ access | 접근 | □ replace | 대체하다 |
| □ individual | 사람, 개인 | □ handwritten | 손으로 쓰여 진 | □ contribution | 기여, 공헌 |
| □ opportunity | 기회 | □ scarce | 희귀한 | □ consequently | 결과적으로 |
| □ participate in | ~에 참여하다 | □ acceptance | 수용, 받아들임 | □ favorable | 호의적인 |
| □ intellectual | 지적인 | □ rapidly | 빠르게 | □ equal | 동등한 |

# 02

다음 글의 요지로 가장 적절한 것은?  71% 고2 06월 모의고사 변형

Having a high follower count on your social media accounts enhances whatever work you are doing in real life. A great comedian spends hours each day working on her skill, but keeps being asked about her Instagram following. Doing so, the comedian with 100,000 followers could promote her upcoming show and increase the chances that people will buy tickets to come see her. This reduces the amount of money spent on promoting the show and makes the producers more likely to choose her again next time. Plenty of people are worried that follower count seems to be more important than talent, but it's really about firing on all cylinders. In today's world of show business, the business part is happening online. You need to adapt to it because those who don't adapt won't succeed.

① 성공하는 데 소셜 미디어에서의 인기가 중요하다.
② 코미디언에게 인기에 대한 지나친 집착은 독이 된다.
③ 온라인 상황과 실제 상황을 구별하는 것이 필요하다.
④ 소비자의 성향을 파악하는 것이 마케팅의 효과를 높인다.
⑤ 공연을 완성하기 위해서는 다양한 분야의 협조가 필요하다.

**➕ 유튜브(YouTube)**
당신(You)과 브라운관(Tube, 텔레비전)의 합성어로, 구글이 운영하는 세계 최대의 동영상 사이트이다. 전 세계 네티즌들이 올리는 동영상 콘텐츠를 공유한다. 2005년 채드 헐리(Chad Hurley), 스티브 첸(Steve Chen), 자웨드 카림(Jawed Karim)이 공동으로 창립했으며, 2006년 구글이 16억 5000만 달러(한화 약 2조)에 이를 인수하였다.

New Words

| | | | | | |
|---|---|---|---|---|---|
| □ account | 계정, 계좌 | □ upcoming | 다가오는 | □ promote | 홍보하다, 촉진시키다 |
| □ enhance | 향상시키다 | □ increase | 높이다, 증가시키다 | □ likely to 동사원형 | ~할 가능성이 있는 |
| □ whatever | 무슨 ~라도; 무엇이든지 | □ chance | 가능성, 기회 | □ seem | ~인 것처럼 보이다 |
| □ spend | (시간 등을) 보내다 | □ reduce | 줄이다 | □ fire on all cylinders | 전력을 다하다 |
| □ skill | 기술 | □ amount | 양 | □ adapt | 적응하다 |

# 03

**글의 흐름으로 보아, 주어진 문장이 들어가기에 가장 적절한 곳은?** 67% 고2 03월 모의고사 변형

> So, when someone is threatening to go to war or trying to justify the war, the news media have to question everything.

As the media offer diverse and opposing views, we can choose the best available option. Let's take the example of going to war. Obviously, war should be the last resort when all other options have failed. ( ① ) They should be providing the most intense scrutiny, so the public can see the other side of things. ( ② ) Otherwise, we might fall victim to unnecessary wars fought for ridiculous reasons, not for the reasons presented by governments. ( ③ ) Unfortunately, the media often fail to perform this crucial role. ( ④ ) Even the large, 'liberal' American media have admitted that they have not always been watchdogs for the public interest. ( ⑤ ) Their own coverage on some major issues looks strikingly one-sided at times.

*scrutiny (면밀한) 조사

**➕ 퓰리처상**
미국 저널리스트인 조셉 퓰리처(Joseph Pulitzer, 1847~1911)의 유언에 의해 1917년에 제정되었으며, 시상식은 5월 말에 열린다. 뉴스·보도사진 등 15개 부문, 문학·음악 7개 부문을 대상으로 인물을 추천받아 수여한다. '로이터' 김경훈 사진기자가 2019년 '브레이킹 뉴스' 부문에서 한국인 최초의 퓰리처 수상자가 되었다.

**New Words**

| | | | | | |
|---|---|---|---|---|---|
| ☐ threaten | 위협하다 | ☐ last resort | 최후의 수단 | ☐ crucial | 중대한, 중요한 |
| ☐ justify | 정당화하다 | ☐ intense | 치열한, 격렬한 | ☐ liberal | 진보적인 |
| ☐ question | 의심하다, 질문하다 | ☐ victim | 희생자 | ☐ admit | 인정하다 |
| ☐ diverse | 다양한 | ☐ ridiculous | 말도 안 되는 | ☐ watchdog | 파수꾼, 감시인 |
| ☐ opposing | 상반된, 반대되는 | ☐ government | 정부 | ☐ coverage | 보도, 방송 |
| ☐ option | 선택(권) | ☐ perform | 수행하다, 공연하다 | ☐ strikingly | 눈에 띄게, 현저히 |

# Vocabulary Review

**01** 다음 주어진 단어를 활용하여 빈칸을 완성하시오.

| adapt | consistently | contribution | access | admit |
|---|---|---|---|---|

(1) She _____ scored the highest grades in class.

(2) He has never _____ that my opinion was better than his.

(3) The students can have _____ to various information online.

(4) The transferred student tried to _____ to the new circumstances.

(5) Sejong the Great made a great _____ with the invention of Hangeul.

**02** 다음 영영풀이에 해당하는 단어를 보기에서 골라 쓰시오.

보기
| suburb | reduce | escalate | replace | government |
|---|---|---|---|---|
| intense | opportunity | justify | public | account |

(1) _____ : all ordinary people

(2) _____ : requiring a lot of effort to do something

(3) _____ : to make or become greater or more serious

(4) _____ : an area on the edge of a large town or city

(5) _____ : to change something to a more proper one

(6) _____ : to show that something is reasonable, right, or true

(7) _____ : the group of people who officially control a country

(8) _____ : an occasion or situation which makes it possible to do something

(9) _____ : an arrangement to use an internet service or bank service as a member

(10) _____ : to become or to make something become smaller in size, amount, etc.

UNIT

# 12 컴퓨터, 인터넷, 교통

주제 소개  현대생활에서 필수적인 역할을 하는 컴퓨터와 인터넷의 발달 과정과 장단점에 관해 설명하고, 인간이 어떻게 상호 교류해야 하는지에 관한 내용이 주로 나온다. 교통은 운송 수단에 관한 것은 물론, 과거에 나타난 교통의 발생과 발달이 현재에 미치는 영향에 관해 주요하게 다룬다.

**Q** 글의 흐름으로 보아, 주어진 문장이 들어가기에 가장 적절한 곳은?  58% 고2 06월 모의고사 변형

> Conversely, a computer cannot make independent decisions; it fails to formulate steps for solving problems if not programmed by humans.

[1]It is vital to remember that computers can only carry out instructions that humans give them. Computers can process data accurately at far greater speeds than people, but they are limited in many aspects. Most importantly, they lack common sense. ( ① ) [2]However, combining the strengths of these machines with those of humans' creates synergy. ( ② ) Synergy occurs when combined resources produce output that exceeds the sum of the outputs of the same resources employed separately. ( ③ ) A computer works quickly and accurately; humans work relatively slowly and make mistakes. ( ④ ) Even with sophisticated artificial intelligence, the initial programming must be done by humans. ( ⑤ ) Therefore, a human-computer combination allows the results of human thought to be changed into efficient processing of large amounts of data.

*sophisticated 정교한

| | | | | | | |
|---|---|---|---|---|---|
| □ conversely | 반대로 | □ aspect | 측면, 양상, 관점 | □ sum | 합, 총합 |
| □ independent | 독립적인 | □ lack | ~이 부족하다 | □ employ | 이용하다, 고용하다 |
| □ formulate | 만들어 내다 | □ combine | 결합하다 | □ relatively | 상대적으로 |
| □ vital | 중요한 | □ resource | 자원, 원천, 자질 | □ artificial | 인공의 |
| □ carry out | 수행하다 | □ output | 산출(량) | □ intelligence | 지능, 지성 |
| □ accurately | 정확히 | □ exceed | 초과하다, 넘다 | □ initial | 초기의, 처음의 |

## Reading Check

빈칸에 들어갈 알맞은 말을 지문에서 찾아 적어 보세요.

| 도입<br>(정의) | • Synergy is the effect of ¹_____ two things to produce a<br>²_____ greater than that of their individual ones. |
|---|---|
| 전개<br>(비교) | • Humans can give computers instructions, have common<br>³_____ and can make ⁴_____ decisions.<br>• Computers can process data accurately, ⁵_____ fast and<br>correctly. |
| 발전<br>(결과) | • What humans think can be changed into much more ⁶_____<br>data conducted by ⁷_____. |

## Analyzing Sentences

❶ **It** is vital **to remember** [**that** computers can only carry out instructions {**that** humans give them}].

⋯ 가주어(It) 진주어(to 부정사)의 구문으로 [ ] 부분에서 that은 명사절 접속사이고, { } 부분에서 that은 목적격 관계대명사이다.

❷ However, **combining the strengths** of these machines with **those** of humans' creates synergy.

⋯ 문장의 주어는 동명사 combining 이며 동사는 creates이다. those는 앞부분의 the strengths와 중복을 피하기 위해 사용되었다.

---

**Background Knowledge**

인공지능(Artificial Intelligence)

인간만이 할 수 있다고 여겨지는 경험과 지식을 바탕으로 문제를 해결하는 능력, 시각 및 음성 인식의 지각 능력, 자연 언어 이해 능력, 자율적으로 움직이는 능력 등을 컴퓨터나 전자 기술로 실현하고자 하는 인공 지능의 궁극적인 목표는 사람처럼 생각하고 행동할 수 있는 것이다. 하지만, 인공지능이 수행한 업무의 결과에 대한 윤리적 책임에 관한 문제가 함께 논의되어야 한다.

01

**글의 흐름으로 보아, 주어진 문장이 들어가기에 가장 적절한 곳은?** 48% 고2 09월 모의고사 변형

> However, there have been concerns that cookies may be violating privacy by helping companies or government agencies accumulate personal information.

Favorite websites sometimes welcome users like old friends. Online bookstores greet their customers by name and suggest new books they might want to read. Real estate sites guide their visitors to new properties that have come on the market. ( ① ) These tricks are made possible by cookies. ( ② ) They are small files that an Internet server stores inside individuals' web browsers so that it can remember them. ( ③ ) On the bright side, cookies can greatly benefit individuals. ( ④ ) For example, cookies save users the time spent on entering names and addresses into e-commerce websites every time they make a purchase. ( ⑤ ) Security is another concern; cookies make shared computers far less safe and offer hackers many ways to break into systems.

➕ **파밍(pharming)**
private data(개인 자료)와 farming(기르기)의 합성어로 사용자를 속여 가짜 사이트에 접속하도록 유도하는 사기 수법이다. 사용자는 인터넷 주소를 정확하게 입력하더라도 가짜 사이트로 연결되어 각종 개인정보를 입력하게 된다. 우리가 흔히 알고 있는 피싱(phishing) 사기 수법보다 훨씬 속기 쉽고 위험하다.

| New Words | | | | | |
|---|---|---|---|---|---|
| □ concern | 우려, 염려 | □ real estate | 부동산 | □ enter | 입력하다 |
| □ violate | 침해하다, 위반하다 | □ property | 부동산, 재산 | □ every time | ~할 때마다 |
| □ privacy | 사생활 | □ trick | 기술, 묘기 | □ security | 보안, 안전 |
| □ agency | 기관, 소속사 | □ store | 저장하다; 상점 | □ shared | 공유되는 |
| □ accumulate | 축적하다 | □ benefit | 이익을 주다 | □ far | 훨씬; 먼; 멀리 |
| □ greet | 인사하다 | □ individual | 개인, 사람 | □ break into | ~에 침입하다 |

## 02 다음 글의 밑줄 친 부분 중, 어법상 틀린 것은?

65% 고2 03월 모의고사 변형

Commercial airplanes travel in airways which are similar to roads. Airways have fixed widths and defined altitudes, ① which separate traffic moving in opposite directions. Vertical separation of aircraft enables some flights ② to pass over airports while other processes occur below. Air flights usually travel long distances, and there are two types of travel. One is short periods of intense pilot activity at takeoff and landing; the other is long periods of lower pilot activity in the air, the portion of the flight ③ known as the "long haul." During the long-haul portion of a flight, pilots spend more time assessing aircraft status than ④ searching out nearby planes. This is because collisions between airplanes usually occur in the area surrounding airports, while crashes due to aircraft malfunction ⑤ tends to happen during long-haul flights.

*altitude 고도 **long-haul 장거리비행의

➕ 대권항로(great circle)
지구는 공 모양으로 되어 있기 때문에, 적도 부근에서 좌우로 어느 한 거리와 거리를 직선으로 표시할 경우, 그것을 실제 둥근 모양으로 복귀시킬 때보다 먼 거리가 된다. 대권항로는 항공기 교통을 운영할 때, 극으로 갈수록 거리가 짧아지는 현상을 이용하는 원리로 비행기 시간을 단축하고 연료를 절약하기 위해 사용된다.

| | | | | | |
|---|---|---|---|---|---|
| □ commercial | 민간의, 상업의 | □ direction | 방향, 지시 | □ intense | 고강도의, 집중적인 |
| □ airplane | 항공기, 비행기 | □ vertical | 수직적인, 수직의 | □ assess | 평가하다 |
| □ fixed | 고정된 | □ aircraft | 항공기 | □ status | 상태, 지위 |
| □ width | 폭, 넓이 | □ enable | 가능하게 하다 | □ collision | 충돌 |
| □ defined | 규정된, 정의된 | □ process | 과정; 처리하다 | □ due to | ~로 인한, ~때문인 |
| □ separate | 분리하다 | □ occur | 일어나다 | □ malfunction | 오작동 |
| □ opposite | 반대의 | □ distance | 거리 | □ tend to 동사원형 | ~하는 경향이 있다 |

# 03

정답과 해설 P.24

**글의 흐름으로 보아, 주어진 문장이 들어가기에 가장 적절한 곳은?**  57% 고2 09월 모의고사 변형

> But the examination of the accuracy of information obtained in this way is not a simple matter.

The Internet could offer us the rapid acquisition of new information as an aid to thinking. ( ① ) But this is more fictional than real. ( ② ) Actually, the simple act of typing a few words into google will virtually instantaneously produce links related to the topic at hand. ( ③ ) What we often get are no more than abstract summaries of long articles. ( ④ ) Hence, I suspect that the number of downloads of any given scientific paper has little relevance to the number of times people have been reading the entire article from beginning to end. ( ⑤ ) If you want to think of something more serious, then I recommend that you disconnect the Internet, phone, and other devices and try spending twenty-four hours in absolute solitude.

*solitude 고독

BIG DATA

➕ 빅데이터(big data)
대규모의 정보를 추출하고 결과를 분석, 비교하여 더 큰 가치를 창출하는 기술을 뜻한다. 통계나 수치 등 등 기존의 정형화된 정보뿐 아니라 텍스트, 이미지, 오디오, 로그기록 등 비정형 정보 모두를 다룬다. 최근에는 모바일기기, SNS, 사물인터넷 확산 등으로 다루어야 할 정보의 양이 기하급수적으로 늘어나고 있다.

**New Words**

| | | | | | |
|---|---|---|---|---|---|
| □ examination | 조사, 연구 | □ actually | 사실, 실제로 | □ hence | 따라서, 그러므로 |
| □ accuracy | 정확성 | □ virtually | 거의, 사실상 | □ suspect | 생각하다, 의심하다 |
| □ obtain | 얻다, 획득하다 | □ instantaneously | 즉각적으로 | □ relevance | 관련, 적절성 |
| □ rapid | 신속한, 빠른 | □ at hand | 다루고 있는, 가까운 | □ entire | 전체의, 완전한 |
| □ acquisition | 습득, 획득 | □ no more than | ~에 지나지 않는 | □ disconnect | (연락을) 끊다 |
| □ aid | 조력자, 도움 | □ abstract | 추상적인 | □ device | 장치, 기계 |
| □ fictional | 허구적인, 지어낸 | □ article | 글, 기사 | □ absolute | 절대적인, 확실한 |

**01** 다음 주어진 단어를 활용하여 빈칸을 완성하시오.

| accumulate | entire | combine | occur | exceed |

(1) The artists demanded _____ freedom of expression.

(2) The company has finally _____ the sales of last year.

(3) This pond _____ organic matter and absorbs carbon.

(4) Water is formed when hydrogen and oxygen are _____.

(5) Yesterday several traffic accidents _____ in our neighborhood.

**02** 다음 영영풀이에 해당하는 단어를 보기에서 골라 쓰시오.

보기  commercial   malfunction   independent   vertical   security
collision   abstract   property   suspect   artificial

(1) _____ : a building or piece of land, or both together

(2) _____ : at an angle of 90° to a horizontal surface or line

(3) _____ : to think or believe something to be true or probable

(4) _____ : made by people, often as a copy of something natural

(5) _____ : used for selling goods or providing services for money

(6) _____ : a failure to work or operate in a correct or proper way

(7) _____ : not controlled in any way by other people, events, or things

(8) _____ : existing as an idea, feeling, or quality, not as a material object

(9) _____ : an accident that happens when two vehicles hit each other with force

(10) _____ : protection of a person, building, organization, or country against threats

주 제 소 개    인간의 심리와 행동을 이해하는데 도움을 주는 현상과 실험, 연구에 관한 내용을 다룬다. 사회 활동의 핵심은 인간과 인간의 관계에 있기 때문에 올바른 사회 활동을 위한 인간관계를 어떻게 형성해야 하고, 과거에는 타인과의 관계가 어떠했는지 등에 관한 내용이 주를 이룬다.

**Q** 다음 글의 밑줄 친 부분 중, 문맥상 낱말의 쓰임이 적절하지 않은 것은? 37% 고2 09월 모의고사 지문/문제 변형

The Pratfall Effect is a phenomenon of social psychology. It states that individuals' perceived attractiveness increases or decreases after they make a mistake, depending on their ① perceived competence. ❶Celebrities are generally considered to be competent individuals, and often even thought of as flawless or perfect in certain aspects. So, if they commit blunders, it will make their humanness endearing to others. ❷Basically, those who never make mistakes are perceived as being less ② attractive than those who make occasional mistakes. Perfection ③ creates a perceived distance that the general public cannot relate to, making those who never make mistakes perceived as being difficult to approach. However, this can also have the ④ similar effect. That is, if people known to be perceived average or less than average competent make a mistake, they will be ⑤ less attractive and likable to others.

*blunder (부주의하거나 어리석은) 실수

New Words

☐ phenomenon  현상
☐ state  (분명히) 말하다; 상태
☐ perceived  인지된
☐ attractiveness  매력(도)
☐ depend on  ~에 달려있다
☐ competence  능력

☐ celebrity  유명 인사, 연예인
☐ consider  여기다, 간주하다
☐ flawless  흠이 없는, 완벽한
☐ certain  어떤, 확실한
☐ aspect  면, 측면, 관점
☐ commit  ~을 저지르다

☐ endearing  사랑 받는
☐ occasional  가끔의
☐ relate to  ~와 관련짓다
☐ approach  다가가다; 접근
☐ average  평균의; 평균
☐ likable  호감적인

## Reading Check

**빈칸에 들어갈 알맞은 말을 지문에서 찾아 적어 보세요.**

| 주제 | The Pratfall Effect refers to a changing in ¹_____ according to perceived ability |
|---|---|
| 비교 ① | **Celebrities**<br>• are seen as capable and ²_____<br>• are found difficult to ³_____<br>  → will be seen as more attractive when they make ⁴_____ |
| 비교 ② | **Common people**<br>• are thought to be ⁵_____ attractive<br>  → will be less ⁶_____ and likable when people average or less than average make mistakes |

## Analyzing Sentences

❶ Celebrities **are** generally **considered to be** competent individuals, ~.

⋯▸ 수동태 be considered to 동사원형(~으로 여겨지다, 간주되다)의 형태로 이루어진 문장이다.

❷ Basically, **those** [**who** never make mistakes] are perceived **as** being less ~ than **those** [**who** make occasional mistakes].

⋯▸ those는 [ ] 부분인 주격 관계대명사절의 수식을 받는 the people(사람들)이라는 뜻이며, as는 전치사로 쓰여 be동사의 동명사인 being으로 연결되었다.

---

**Background Knowledge**

**가스라이팅(Gaslighting)**

1938년 만들어진 연극 '가스등(Gas Light)'에서 유래한 용어로 가정, 학교, 연인 등 주로 친밀한 관계에서 이뤄지는 경우가 많다. 상대방의 심리나 상황을 교묘하게 조작해 판단력을 잃게 하는 정서적 학대 행위이다. 가스라이팅을 당한 사람은 자신의 판단력을 믿지 못하게 되어 가해자에게 점차 의존하게 된다. 이성 관계나 종교 등 맹신과 권위를 통해 상대방을 정신적으로 통제하고 억압하려 할 때 악용된다.

## 01 다음 빈칸에 들어갈 말로 가장 적절한 것은?

39% 고2 11월 모의고사 변형

Most research in psychology was based on the assumption that humans are driven by base motivations such as egoistic self-interest and the pursuit of simple pleasures. Since many psychologists began with that assumption, they inadvertently designed research studies that supported their own thinking. As a result, the dominant view of humanity in psychology was that people barely keep their aggressive tendencies in check and manage to live in social groups out of motivated self-interest. Sigmund Freud and the early behaviorists believed humans were motivated primarily by _____. Social interaction is possible only by exerting control over those baser emotions. Thus it is always vulnerable to eruptions of violence, greed, and selfishness. The fact that humans actually live together in society has traditionally been seen as a weak arrangement that is closely exposed to violence.

\*inadvertently 무심코 \*\*vulnerable 취약한, 연약한

① ethical ideas     ② selfish drives     ③ rational thoughts
④ extrinsic rewards     ⑤ social punishments

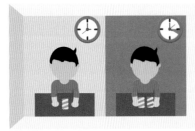

**➕ 마시멜로 실험**(marshmallow experiment)
아이의 절제력이 미래의 성공과 관계가 있다는 것을 알아보는 실험으로 스탠포드 대학의 심리학자 월터 미쉘(W. Mischel)과 연구진에 의해 진행됐다. 아이들이 아무도 없는 상황에서 15분 동안 마시멜로를 먹지 않을 수 있는지 관찰했다. 미쉘은 15년 후 아이들을 다시 만나 마시멜로를 먹지 않고 참았던 아이들의 성공 가능성이 크다고 발표했다.

**New Words**

| | | | | | |
|---|---|---|---|---|---|
| □ be based on | ~에 바탕을 두다 | □ dominant | 지배적인, 우세한 | □ exert | ~을 가하다, 행사하다 |
| □ assumption | 가정 | □ barely | 가까스로 거의 ~하지 않는 | □ violence | 폭력(성) |
| □ base | 저급한; 기반 | □ keep ~ in check | ~을 억제하다 | □ greed | 탐욕 |
| □ motivation | 동기 | □ aggressive | 공격적인 | □ selfishness | 이기심 |
| □ egoistic | 이기적인 | □ manage to 동사원형 | 그럭저럭 ~하다 | □ arrangement | 합의, 협정 |
| □ pursuit | 추구 | □ primarily | 주로 | □ be exposed to | ~에 노출되다 |

## 02

**Patrick Arbore에 관한 다음 글의 내용과 일치하지 <u>않는</u> 것은?**  58% 고2 06월 모의고사 지문/문제 변형

Loneliness can creep into your life with age and that's why it's better to find some ways to not be lonely. Patrick Arbore knew this, and he considered meaningful conversation as a valuable way. Arbore, director and founder of Elderly Suicide Prevention, founded the Friendship Line, a 24-hour hotline where volunteers reach out to potentially suicidal seniors. He says, "I feel a great joy as the listener when someone really hopes for connection." Arbore remembers an old man, who spoke with him on the Friendship Line at a time when he wanted to end his life. After some time he said to him, "I am no longer thinking about suicide because people care about me." Arbore found this exchange profound. He says, "Our work is really quite simple. It's connection and care."

*profound 심오한

① 외롭지 않기 위한 방법을 찾는 것이 좋다는 것을 알았다.
② 노인 자살 방지 단체의 관리자이자 설립자였다.
③ 누군가가 진정한 관계를 원할 때 들어주는 사람으로서 기뻐했다.
④ 자신의 인생을 끝내려고 할 때 노인과 전화로 상담을 했다.
⑤ 연락을 취할 수 있는 교류와 관심이 매우 중요하다고 깨달았다.

**➕ 외로움 유전자**
유전자 역시 외로움을 유발할 수 있는 요인으로 첫 전장 유전체 (genome-wide) 연관성 연구(association study)는 유전자가 외로 움을 얼마나 느낄지를 결정하지만, 개인의 경험과 환경보다는 그 요소가 적은 14~27%로 보았다. 그러나 이전의 연구에서는 외로움의 37~55% 정도를 유전으로 보기도 했다.

---

New Words

| | | | | | |
|---|---|---|---|---|---|
| ☐ creep into | ~에 스며들다, 기어가다 | ☐ director | 관리자, 감독 | ☐ connection | 연결 |
| ☐ lonely | 외로운 | ☐ prevention | 예방, 방지 | ☐ end | ~을 끝내다; 끝 |
| ☐ consider | 여기다, 간주하다 | ☐ found | 설립하다 | ☐ no longer | 더 이상 ~하지 않는 |
| ☐ meaningful | 의미 있는 | ☐ reach out | 연락을 취하다 | ☐ suicide | 자살; 자살하다 |
| ☐ conversation | 대화 | ☐ potentially | 잠재적으로 | ☐ exchange | 교류, 교환 |
| ☐ valuable | 가치 있는 | ☐ senior | 노인, 고령자 | ☐ care | 관심, 돌봄 |

## 03 다음 글의 밑줄 친 부분 중, 어법상 틀린 것은?

68% 고3 06월 모의고사 변형

People from more individualistic cultures seem motivated to maintain self-focused agency or control ① <u>as</u> these serve as the basis of their self-worth. They believe individual successes ② <u>depending</u> primarily on their own abilities and actions. In this way, the use of control is ultimately concentrated on the individual, whether by influencing the environment or trying to accept their circumstances. The independent self may be more ③ <u>driven</u> to cope by appealing to a sense of agency or control. People from more interdependent cultures, however, tend to be less focused on issues of individual success and more motivated towards group goals and harmony. Research has shown ④ <u>that</u> East Asians prefer to receive more social support instead of seeking personal control. Therefore, people ⑤ <u>who</u> hold a more interdependent character might like to cope in a way that promotes harmony in relationships.

➕ **밴드왜건 효과(band wagon effect)**
물건을 구매하는 등의 경제적 판단과 행동을 할 때 유행과 다수의 인기를 좇아가는 현상을 뜻한다. 역마차에서 힌트를 얻은 밴드왜건(band wagon)은 악대를 선두에 세워서 다닌 운송수단으로 많은 사람들을 선동해 몰고 다녔다. 기업에서는 구매를 부추기는 마케팅 기법으로, 정치에서는 선거의 도구로 활용하기도 한다.

**New Words**

| | | | | | |
|---|---|---|---|---|---|
| ☐ individualistic | 개인주의적인 | ☐ ultimately | 궁극적으로, 결국 | ☐ cope | 대처하다 |
| ☐ motivated | 동기를 받는 | ☐ be concentrated on | ~에게 집중되다 | ☐ appeal to | ~에 호소하다 |
| ☐ maintain | 유지하다 | ☐ whether | ~이든 아니든 | ☐ prefer | 선호하다 |
| ☐ self-focused | 자기중심의 | ☐ influence | 영향을 주다; 영향 | ☐ seek | 찾다, 추구하다 |
| ☐ agency | 주체성, (~의) 힘 | ☐ accept | 받아들이다 | ☐ interdependent | 상호의존적인 |
| ☐ as the basis of | ~의 토대로서 | ☐ circumstance | 환경, 상황 | ☐ character | 성격, 인물 |
| ☐ self-worth | 자아 존중감 | ☐ independent | 독립적인, 자주적인 | | |

**01** 다음 주어진 단어를 활용하여 빈칸을 완성하시오.

consider    depend on    potentially    found    exert

(1) The students were _____ to be very diligent.

(2) The businessman has _____ a charity with his money.

(3) The government will _____ every effort to restore the facility.

(4) I think that a _____ dangerous situation will come soon.

(5) Most advertising revenue _____ how many people could see an ad.

**02** 다음 영영풀이에 해당하는 단어를 보기에서 골라 쓰시오.

보기    violence    valuable    influence    celebrity    average
exchange    conversation    prefer    motivation    competence

(1) _____ : important, useful, or beneficial

(2) _____ : the ability to do something well

(3) _____ : considered to be typical or usual

(4) _____ : a talk between two or more people

(5) _____ : actions or words that are intended to hurt people

(6) _____ : to like, choose, or want one thing rather than another

(7) _____ : someone who is famous, especially in the entertainment business

(8) _____ : to change how someone or something develops, behaves, or thinks

(9) _____ : the act of giving something to someone and getting something in return

(10) _____ : willingness to do something, or something that causes such willingness

# UNIT 14 정치, 경제

주제 소개　한 나라의 체제를 유지시켜 주는 정치적 환경이나 제도 등이 자주 언급되며, 지도자의 생애와 자질 등도 소개된다. 다양한 경제 현상을 현 상황과 비교해서 살펴보면서, 경제가 인간의 생활에 미치는 영향 등을 설명하는 내용이 주를 이룬다. 수능에서는 빈칸 완성, 글의 요지, 문장 삽입 등의 유형으로 주로 출제된다.

---

**58% 고2 06월 모의고사 변형**

**Q** 다음 글의 내용을 한 문장으로 요약하고자 한다. 빈칸 (A), (B)에 들어갈 말로 가장 적절한 것은?

　　Contact among groups tends to reduce stereotyping and create favorable attitudes if it is backed by social norms that promote equality. If the norms support openness, friendliness, and mutual respect, ❶the contact has a greater chance of changing attitudes and reducing prejudice than if they do not. Intergroup contact supported by an outside authority or by established customs is more likely to produce positive changes than unsupported contact. Without this institutional support, members in the group may hesitate to interact with outsiders because they feel that doing so is simply inappropriate. With the presence of institutional support, however, contact between groups is more likely to be seen as appropriate, expected, and worthwhile. ❷For example, there is evidence that students were more highly motivated in classes conducted by some teachers. In fact, they were those who didn't oppose, but supported desegregation.

*desegregation 인종 차별 폐지

↓

> Backed by social norms which pursue intergroup equality, intergroup contact tends to weaken ＿＿＿(A)＿＿＿ more, when it is led by ＿＿＿(B)＿＿＿ support.

|  | (A) | (B) |  | (A) | (B) |
|---|---|---|---|---|---|
| ① | bias | organizational | ② | bias | individualized |
| ③ | bias | financial | ④ | balance | organizational |
| ⑤ | balance | individualized |  |  |  |

---

**New Words**

□ contact　접촉, 연락　　□ equality　평등　　□ institutional　제도적인, 제도화된
□ stereotyping　고정관념　　□ mutual　상호의, 서로간의　　□ hesitate　꺼려하다, 주저하다
□ norm　규범, 기준　　□ prejudice　편견　　□ oppose　반대하다

## Reading Check

빈칸에 들어갈 알맞은 말을 지문에서 찾아 적어 보세요.

| 주제 | The impact of reducing prejudice through ¹_____ _____ |
|------|------|
| 사회적<br>규범의 효과 | Supported contact between groups ~.<br><br>• decrease ²_____ and create favorable attitudes<br><br>• has a chance of changing attitudes and reducing ³_____<br><br>• makes ⁴_____ changes in groups supported by institutions |

## Analyzing Sentences

❶ ~ , the contact has a greater chance **of changing** attitudes **and reducing** prejudice **than if** they do not.

⋯▸ 전치사 of 다음에 동명사 changing과 reducing이 등위접속사 and를 기준으로 병렬구조로 연결되어 있다. 접속사 than 뒤에 if절이 사용되어 '~한다면 보다'로 해석된다.

❷ For example, there is **evidence that** students were more highly motivated in **classes conducted** by some teachers.

⋯▸ that은 앞의 evidence(증거)를 설명하기 위해 사용된 명사절 접속사(동격)이며 과거분사 conducted는 classes를 수식하고 있다.

---

**Background<br>Knowledge**

**라포(rapport)**

'rapport(관계, 친밀감)'에서 유래한 용어로, 교육이나 상담을 진행하기 전, 신뢰와 친근감을 만드는 과정을 뜻한다. 상담, 치료, 교육 등은 특성상 상호협조가 중요한데, 라포는 이를 충족시켜주는 원동력이 된다. 라포를 형성하기 위해서는 상대방의 감정, 사고, 경험을 이해할 수 있는 공감대 형성을 위한 노력이 중요하다. 요즘은 교육이나 상담 이외에 다양한 인간관계와 사회생활의 향상을 위해서도 라포라는 용어가 사용된다.

# 01 다음 빈칸에 들어갈 말로 가장 적절한 것은?

47% 고2 11월 모의고사 변형

Veblen goods are named after Thorstein Veblen, who constructed the theory of "conspicuous consumption." Veblen goods seem strange because demand for them increases as their price rises. According to Veblen, these goods must signal high status. A willingness to pay higher prices is due to a desire to show off wealth rather than to acquire better quality. A true Veblen good, therefore, might not be noticeably higher quality than lower-priced one. If the price falls so much that _____, the rich will stop buying it. There is much evidence of this behavior in the markets for luxury cars, champagne, watches, and so on. The seller might experience a temporary increase in sales due to a reduction in prices, but soon sales will begin to decrease.

*conspicuous 과시적인

① the government starts to get involved in the industry
② manufacturers finally decide not to supply the market
③ the law of supply and demand does not work anymore
④ there is no quality competition remaining in the market
⑤ it is no longer high enough to exclude the less well off

**➕ 스놉 효과(Snob effect)**
물건을 구매할 때 구매자가 남과 다른 개성을 추구하려는 의사 결정 현상을 말한다. 영어 'snob(잘난 척 하는 사람, 속물)'에서 유래했으며, 줄곧 사용하던 물건도 남들이 사용하여 대중화가 되면 더 이상 구매하지 않는다. 인기와 유행에 따라 물건을 사려는 밴드왜건 효과(bandwagon effect)와 정반대의 구매 심리현상이라 할 수 있다.

**New Words**

| | | | | | |
|---|---|---|---|---|---|
| □ be named after | ~의 이름을 따서 짓다 | □ status | 지위, 상태 | □ noticeably | 눈에 띄게 |
| □ theory | 이론 | □ willingness | 의사, 의지 | □ evidence | 증거 |
| □ consumption | 소비 | □ desire | 욕망; 바라다 | □ temporary | 일시적인, 임시의 |
| □ goods | 상품, 물건 | □ show off | 뽐내다, 자랑하다 | □ involved | 관여하는 |
| □ demand | 수요; 요구하다 | □ A rather than B | B라기 보다는 A | □ remaining | 남아 있는 |

맨처음 수능 주제별 독해 2

56% 고2 04월 모의고사 변형

## 02

다음 글의 내용을 한 문장으로 요약하고자 한다. 빈칸 (A), (B)에 들어갈 말로 가장 적절한 것은?

Some developing countries which are rich in natural resources tend to depend excessively on their natural resources. It generates a lower variety of production and a lower rate of growth. Resource abundance in itself need not do any harm; it could even be a blessing. As a matter of fact, many countries have abundant natural resources and have tried to overcome dependence on them by diversifying their economic activity. Such is the case of Canada, Australia, and the US, to name the most important countries. But some developing countries are trapped in their dependence on large natural resources. They suffer from a series of problems which restrict their development. That is because a heavy reliance on natural capital tends to exclude other types of capital and thereby interfere with economic growth.

↓

Depending on rich natural resources without ＿＿＿(A)＿＿＿ economic activities can be a ＿＿＿(B)＿＿＿ to economic growth.

|  | (A) | (B) |  | (A) | (B) |
|---|---|---|---|---|---|
| ① | varying | …… barrier | ② | varying | …… shortcut |
| ③ | limiting | …… challenge | ④ | limiting | …… barrier |
| ⑤ | connecting | …… shortcut |  |  |  |

➕ 희토류(rare earth elements)

원소 주기율표 상에 있는 17개 화학 원소의 통칭으로, 스칸듐(Sc)과 이트륨(Y), 란타넘(La)부터 루테튬(Lu)까지의 란타넘족 원소들로 이루어진 광물을 말한다. 첨단산업 제품 생산에 없어서는 안 되는 원료로 중국이 생산량의 90% 이상을 차지하고 있다.

**New Words**

| | | | | | |
|---|---|---|---|---|---|
| ☐ developing country | 개발도상국 | ☐ in itself | 그 자체로 | ☐ restrict | 제한하다 |
| ☐ natural resource | 천연자원 | ☐ blessing | 축복 | ☐ exclude | 배제하다 |
| ☐ excessively | 지나치게 | ☐ overcome | 극복하다 | ☐ capital | 자본, 수도 |
| ☐ generate | 발생시키다 | ☐ diversify | 다양화하다 | ☐ thereby | 그로 인해 |
| ☐ abundance | 풍요, 풍부 | ☐ trapped | (덫에) 갇힌 | ☐ interfere with | ~을 방해하다 |

# 03

**글의 흐름으로 보아, 주어진 문장이 들어가기에 가장 적절한 곳은?**  40% 고3 06월 모의고사 변형

> The leaders might have great difficulty coping with too many inputs, such as e-mails, meetings, and phone calls, that only distract and confuse their thinking.

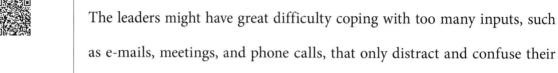

Clarity is often difficult for a leader to obtain. Concerns of the present seem larger than those farther away. ( ① ) Some decisions by leaders present great complexity because there are many variables which must come together a certain way for the leaders to succeed. ( ② ) Alternatively, leaders' information might be only fragmentary, causing them to fill in the gaps with assumptions. ( ③ ) Also, the merits of leaders' important decisions typically are not very clear. ( ④ ) So those decisions have to involve assigning weights to competing interests, and then determining which one is better than the other. ( ⑤ ) Even so, the result is still unclear; it is like saying that Beethoven is a better composer than Brahms.

\*fragmentary 단편적인

**➕ 케네디 스쿨(Kennedy School)**
하버드대학교에 있는 케네디 스쿨은 '케네디 공공정책 대학원' 또는 'HKS' 라고 불린다. 1936년 미국인 사업가 루셔스 리타워(Lucius N. Littauer)가 기부한 200만 달러의 기금을 바탕으로 설립되었고, 1966년에 케네디 전 대통령의 이름을 따서 케네디 스쿨로 이름을 변경했다. 우리나라 출신의 졸업생으로는 반기문 전 UN사무총장이 있다.

New Words

| | | | | | |
|---|---|---|---|---|---|
| ☐ cope with | ~을 다루다 | ☐ present | 현재(의); 제시하다 | ☐ assumption | 가정 |
| ☐ input | 정보, 입력 | ☐ complexity | 복잡성 | ☐ merit | 가치, 혜택 |
| ☐ distract | 흐트러뜨리다 | ☐ variable | 변수; 다양한 | ☐ assign | 부여하다, 배정하다 |
| ☐ confuse | 혼란스럽게 하다 | ☐ certain | 어떤, 확실한 | ☐ determine | 결정하다, 결심하다 |
| ☐ concern | 우려, 관심 | ☐ alternatively | 그게 아니면 | ☐ composer | 작곡가 |

**01** 다음 주어진 단어를 활용하여 빈칸을 완성하시오.

hesitate     assign     exclude     restrict     mutual

(1) The prisoners were _____ to separate rooms.

(2) We discovered a _____ interest in art by chance.

(3) Leaders should not _____ the possibility of negotiation.

(4) They had to _____ the amount of money they spent each month.

(5) Please don't _____ to contact me if you have any questions.

**02** 다음 영영풀이에 해당하는 단어를 보기에서 골라 쓰시오.

보기    evidence    temporary    assumption    blessing    norm
confuse    capital    generate    determine    demand

(1) _____: to make a strong decision

(2) _____: not lasting or needed for very long

(3) _____: a need for something to be sold or supplied

(4) _____: something that is extremely lucky or makes you happy

(5) _____: to produce or create something such as a profits, sales, etc.

(6) _____: something that you accept as true without question or proof

(7) _____: a way of behaving or doing things that most people agree with

(8) _____: one or more reasons for believing that something is or is not true

(9) _____: money needed for producing more wealth or for starting a new business

(10) _____: to mix up someone's ideas, or to make something difficult to understand

주 제 소 개 주로 사람의 심리 또는 사회적 현상, 민주주의, 사회 문제에 관해 논의하는 분야로 수능에서는 글의 주제, 제목, 요지뿐만 아니라 함의 추론, 빈칸 완성 유형으로 많이 출제된다. 신문이나 뉴스 등에 자주 등장하는 다양한 사회 문제들에 관심을 가지고 정보를 파악할 필요가 있다.

42% 고2 11월 모의고사 변형

**Q** 다음 글의 내용을 한 문장으로 요약하고자 한다. 빈칸 (A), (B)에 들어갈 말로 가장 적절한 것은?

❶Power distance is the term which is used to represent how widely an unequal distribution of power is accepted by the members of a culture. It relates to the degree to which the less powerful members of a society accept their inequality in power and consider it the norm. In cultures where there is high acceptance of power distance (e.g., India), people are not regarded as equals, and everyone has a clearly defined or allocated place in the social hierarchy. In cultures where there is low acceptance of power distance (e.g., Finland), people believe that inequality should be minimal, and a hierarchical division is seen as one of convenience only. In these cultures, there is more fluidity within the social hierarchy, and ❷it is relatively easy for individuals to move up the social hierarchy based on their individual efforts and achievements. ↓

*hierarchy 계층, 계급

> Unlike cultures with high acceptance of power distance, where members are more _____(A)_____ to accept inequality, cultures with low acceptance allow more _____(B)_____ within the social hierarchy.

| (A) | (B) | | (A) | (B) |
|---|---|---|---|---|
| ① willing | ······ mobility | | ② willing | ······ assistance |
| ③ reluctant | ······ resistance | | ④ reluctant | ······ flexibility |
| ⑤ afraid | ······ openness | | | |

**New Words**

| □ term | 용어 | □ norm | 규범 | □ fluidity | 유동성 |
|---|---|---|---|---|---|
| □ distribution | 분배 | □ define | 규정[정의]하다 | □ mobility | 이동, 이동성 |
| □ relate to | ~와 관계가 있다 | □ allocate | 할당하다 | □ reluctant | 꺼리는 |
| □ inequality | 불평등 | □ convenience | 편의, 편리 | □ resistance | 저항, 반대 |

● **Reading Check**

빈칸에 들어갈 알맞은 말을 지문에서 찾아 적어 보세요.

| 정의 | Power distance is how widely a(n) ¹_____ _____ of power is accepted by people. |
|---|---|
| 비교 ① | **High acceptance of power distance**<br>• people not regarded as ²_____<br>• a clearly ³_____ or allocated place in the social hierarchy |
| 비교 ② | **Low acceptance of power distance**<br>• people's belief that inequality should be ⁴_____<br>• a hierarchical division seen as one of ⁵_____<br>• more ⁶_____ within the social hierarchy |

● **Analyzing Sentences**

❶ Power distance is the term [**which** is used to represent {**how** widely an unequal distribution of power is accepted by the members of a culture}].

⋯▶ [ ]는 the term을 수식하는 관계절이며 그 안에 { }는 represent의 목적어 역할을 하는 명사절이다.

❷ ~ , and it is relatively easy **for** individuals [**to move up** the social hierarchy {**that** is based on their individual efforts and achievements}].

⋯▶ it은 가주어, for individuals는 의미상 주어, [ ]는 진주어이고, 그 안에 있는 { }는 앞에 있는 선행사 the social hierarchy를 수식하는 관계절이다.

---

**Background Knowledge**

**문화 차원 이론(cultural dimensions theory)**
네덜란드 림뷔르흐 대학교의 조직 인류학 연구자인 기어트 홉스테더(Geert Hofstede)는 한 사회의 문화가 구성원의 가치관에 미치는 영향과 그로 인한 행동의 연관성을 개인주의와 집단주의, 불확실성 회피, 권력 격차, 남성성과 여성성, 장기 지향성 등의 요인을 통해 분석했다. 이는 문화 차이를 계량화한 최초의 시도로 평가된다.

## 01 다음 글의 밑줄 친 부분 중, 문맥상 낱말의 쓰임이 적절하지 <u>않은</u> 것은?

57% 고2 06월 모의고사 변형

Employers with a variety of economic concepts are taking advantage of the law so that they can reap more benefits. Historical evidence points to workers who are exploited by employers in the ① <u>absence</u> of adequate laws. This means that workers are not always compensated for their ② <u>contributions</u>, for their increased productivity, as economic theory would suggest. Employers will be able to exploit workers if they are not legally ③ <u>controlled</u>. As a result, the minimum wage laws may be the only way to inhibit many employees from working at wages which are ④ <u>above</u> the poverty line. This point of view means that minimum wage laws are a source of correcting for existing market failure, while they are ⑤ <u>enhancing</u> the power of markets to create efficient results.

➕ 시장 실패(Market failure)
시장자율기구인 '보이지 않는 손(invisible hand)'에 맡겨져도 효율적 자원 배분이 이루어지지 않는 상황을 말한다. 이때 정부의 개입을 통해 해소하기도 하는데, 독과점 행위 규제, 보조금 지급 및 과징금 부과, 공익사업 추진 등과 같은 정부의 시장 개입을 '보이는 손(visible hand)'이라고 한다.

New Words

| | | | | | |
|---|---|---|---|---|---|
| □ employer | 고용주 | □ historical | 역사적인 | □ productivity | 생산성 |
| □ economic | 경제의, 경제적인 | □ point | 가리키다 | □ theory | 이론 |
| □ concept | 개념 | □ exploit | 착취하다 | □ wage | 임금 |
| □ take advantage of | 활용[이용]하다 | □ absence | 부재 | □ poverty | 빈곤 |
| □ reap | 받다, 거두다 | □ adequate | 적절한 | □ exist | 존재하다 |
| □ benefit | 혜택, 수당 | □ compensate for | 보상하다 | □ efficient | 효율적인 |

## 02

정답과 해설 P.29

**다음 글의 주제로 가장 적절한 것은?**

69% 고2 09월 모의고사 변형

Remember that the original idea of a patent was not to reward inventors with monopoly profits, but to encourage them to share their inventions. A certain amount of intellectual property law is plainly necessary in order to achieve this. But it has gone too far. Most patents are now as much about defending monopoly and discouraging rivals as about sharing ideas, which disrupts innovation. Many firms use patents as barriers to entry, and they sue upstart innovators that trespass on their intellectual property even on the way to some other goal. In the years before World War I, aircraft manufacturers tied each other up in patent lawsuits and slowed down innovation until the US government stepped in. Much the same has happened with smartphones and biotechnology today. New entrants have to navigate through "patent thickets" if they want to create new technologies based on existing ones.

*trespass 침해하다

① ways to protect intellectual property
② the side effects of anti-monopoly laws
③ requirements for applying for a patent
④ patent law abuse that hinders innovation
⑤ resources needed for technological innovation

OPEN CONTENT

➕ **공익을 위해 특허권을 등록하지 않은 사례**
빌헬름 뢴트겐(x선을 발견하였으나 원래 있던 것을 발견한 것이기에 온 인류가 공유해야 한다며 특허를 거절), 에드워드 제너(천연두 백신에 대한 특허를 포기하여 전 세계적인 접종으로 박멸에 공헌), 팀 버너스리 (www, url, http를 개발하였지만, 정보는 자유로워야 한다며 특허권을 등록하지 않음) 등이 공익을 위해 특허권을 등록하지 않았다.

New Words

| □ original | 원래의 | □ defend | 옹호하다 | □ sue | 고소하다 |
|---|---|---|---|---|---|
| □ patent | 특허, 특허권 | □ discourage | 단념시키다 | □ aircraft | 항공기 |
| □ monopoly | 독점 | □ disrupt | 방해하다 | □ manufacturer | 제조사 |
| □ profit | 이익 | □ firm | 회사 | □ step in | 개입하다 |
| □ plainly | 분명히 | □ barrier | 장벽 | □ navigate | 나아가다, 항해하다 |

# 03 다음 글의 제목으로 가장 적절한 것은?

67% 고3 06월 모의고사 변형

Racial and ethnic relations in the United States are better today than in the past, but many changes are needed before sports can be a model of inclusion and fairness. The challenges today are different from the ones which were faced twenty years ago, and experience shows that when current challenges are met, a new social situation is created that new challenges emerge in. For instance, once racial and ethnic segregation is eliminated and people come together, they have to learn to live, work, and play with each other in spite of a variety of experiences and cultural perspectives. Meeting this challenge requires a commitment to equal treatment, plus learning about the perspectives of others, understanding how they define and give meaning to the world, and then determining how they build and maintain relationships while respecting differences, making compromises, and supporting one another in the pursuit of goals which may not always be allocated.

*segregation 분리

① Cooperation Lies at the Heart of Sportsmanship
② All for One, One for All: The Power of Team Sports
③ The History of Racial and Ethnic Diversity in Sports
④ Racial and Ethnic Injustice in Sports: Cause and Effect
⑤ On-going Challenges in Sports: Racial and Ethnic Issues

➕ **현대 올림픽의 역사와 정신**
프랑스의 교육가인 쿠베르탱이 유럽 각국의 찬성을 얻은 결과, 1896년 그리스 아테네에서 제1회 올림픽 대회를 개최하였다. 국제대회로서 모습을 갖춘 것은 4회 런던 대회로 마라톤 코스를 정하는 등 체제를 갖추었다. 올림픽은 제 1, 2차 세계대전으로 인해 세 번 중단된 적이 있다.

---

New Words

| | | | | | |
|---|---|---|---|---|---|
| ☐ racial | 인종의, 인종적인 | ☐ current | 현재의 | ☐ determine | 결정[결심]하다 |
| ☐ ethnic | 민족의, 민족적인 | ☐ emerge | 나오다, 등장하다 | ☐ maintain | 유지하다 |
| ☐ inclusion | 통합, 포함 | ☐ eliminate | 제거하다 | ☐ respect | 존중하다 |
| ☐ fairness | 공정성 | ☐ perspective | 관점, 시각 | ☐ compromise | 타협 |
| ☐ challenge | 난제, 도전 | ☐ treatment | 대우 | ☐ allocate | 공유하다, 할당하다 |

**01** 다음 주어진 단어를 활용하여 빈칸을 완성하시오.

| reluctant | economic | benefit | original | racial |
| --- | --- | --- | --- | --- |

(1) The king was _____ to sell the goods to his rival.

(2) The government is hoping for a(n) _____ recovery.

(3) There should be no _____ discrimination in the world from now on.

(4) Even though we lost the _____ picture, we were lucky to have copies.

(5) People receiving unemployment _____ want to get as much as possible.

**02** 다음 영영풀이에 해당하는 단어를 보기에서 골라 쓰시오.

보기
| define | mobility | resistance | exploit | efficient |
| --- | --- | --- | --- | --- |
| monopoly | disrupt | sue | emerge | compromise |

(1) _____ : to obstruct the progress

(2) _____ : to accuse of wrongdoing

(3) _____ : the ability to move freely and easily

(4) _____ : to become apparent or to be revealed

(5) _____ : an agreement or settlement of a dispute

(6) _____ : the refusal to accept or comply with something

(7) _____ : complete power or control over a person or situation

(8) _____ : to make full use of and derive benefit from a resource

(9) _____ : to precisely state or describe the nature, scope, or meaning

(10) _____ : capable of maximizing productivity at no expense of extra resources

**주 제 소 개**    운동이 신체에 끼치는 영향이나 영양소의 역할, 질병 등에 대해 다루는 분야로 수능에서는 글의 주제, 제목, 요지, 함의 추론, 그리고 빈칸 완성 문제로 가장 많이 출제되는 경향이 있다. 그 밖에 다양한 유형으로도 출제되니 의학과 관련된 상식과 관련 단어들을 학습하며 수능에 대비해야 한다.

**Q**    글의 흐름으로 보아, 주어진 문장이 들어가기에 가장 적절한 곳은?    68% 고2 04월 모의고사 변형

> In some cases, their brains had ceased to function altogether.

Of all the medical accomplishments of the 1960s, ❶the most widely publicized was the first heart transplant, performed by the South African surgeon Christiaan Barnard in 1967. ( ① ) The patient's death 18 days later did not weaken the spirits of those who welcomed a new era of medicine — with its attendant ethical dilemmas. ( ② ) The ability to perform heart transplants was linked to the development of respirators, and they had been introduced to hospitals in the 1950s. ( ③ ) Respirators could save many lives, but not all those whose hearts kept beating ever recovered other critical functions. ( ④ ) ❷The realization that such patients could be a source of organs for transplantation led to the establishment of the Harvard Brain Death Committee, and to its recommendation that the absence of all "discernible central nervous system activity" should be "a new criterion for death." ( ⑤ ) The recommendation has since been adopted, with some modifications, almost everywhere.

*respirator 인공호흡기 **discernible 식별 가능한 ***criterion 기준

**New Words**

| | | | | | |
|---|---|---|---|---|---|
| ☐ cease | 멈추다 | ☐ era | 시대 | ☐ recommendation | 권고 |
| ☐ function | 기능하다; 기능 | ☐ attendant | 수반하는 | ☐ absence | 부재 |
| ☐ accomplishment | 성취 | ☐ ethical | 윤리적인 | ☐ central nervous system | 중추 신경계 |
| ☐ the publicized | 알려진 것 | ☐ dilemma | 진퇴양난, 문제 | | |
| ☐ transplant | 이식 | ☐ critical | 중요한 | ☐ adopt | 채택하다 |
| ☐ surgeon | 외과 의사 | ☐ organ | 장기 | ☐ modification | 수정 |
| ☐ spirit | 마음, 정신 | | | | |

빈칸에 들어갈 알맞은 말을 지문에서 찾아 적어 보세요.

| 도입 | • The first heart transplant is one of the most well-known medical <br> ¹_____ of the 1960s. |
|---|---|
| 전개 | • The death did not affect the people who welcomed a new <br> ²_____ of medicine. <br><br> • Heart transplants were linked to the ³_____ of respirators. <br><br> • Not all those ⁴_____ hearts kept beating ⁵_____ other functions. |
| 발전 | • The patients could be a source of organs for transplantation. <br><br> • The ⁶_____ of "discernible central nervous system activity" should be "a new criterion for ⁷_____." |

❶ ~ the most widely publicized was the first heart transplant, [**performed by** the South African surgeon Christiaan Barnard in 1967].

⋯▶ [ ]는 the first heart transplant를 뒤에서 수식해주는 과거분사구이다.

❷ The realization [**that** such patients could be a source of organs for transplantation] led to the establishment of the Harvard Brain Death Committee, ~.

⋯▶ [ ]는 The realization의 내용을 구체적으로 설명해주는 동격의 that절이다.

**Background Knowledge**

**사망의 기준과 판단**

과거에는 심장이 정지하는 것을 죽음의 기준으로 보았다. 이후 심폐소생술과 제세동기가 개발되어 심장이 정지해도 빠른 처치로 소생이 가능하다는 게 알려지면서 1960년대 이후 뇌파와 호흡계까지 정지한 완전한 뇌사를 죽음의 기준으로 삼고 있다. 하지만 하버드대 데이비드 싱클레어 교수는 미래에는 현재의 사망 기준과 정의가 완전히 뒤바뀔 수 있다고 주장한다.

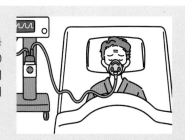

## 01 주어진 글 다음에 이어질 글의 순서로 가장 적절한 것은?

58% 고2 11월 모의고사 변형

Some fad diets might have you running a caloric deficit, and although this might promote weight loss, it has no effect on improving body composition, and could actually lead to a loss of muscle mass.

(A) Timing is also important. By eating the right combinations of these key macronutrients at strategic intervals throughout the day, we can help our bodies to heal and grow much faster.

(B) Your body also needs the right balance of key macronutrients so as to heal and grow stronger. These macronutrients, which include protein, carbohydrates, and healthy fats, can help your body maximize its ability to repair, rebuild, and grow stronger.

(C) Calorie restriction can slow your metabolism and reduce your energy levels significantly. Controlling caloric intake to deliver the appropriate amount of calories so that the body has the energy it needs to function and heal is the only appropriate approach.

*fad (일시적인) 유행 **macronutrient 다량 영양소

① (A) − (C) − (B)　　② (B) − (A) − (C)　　③ (B) − (C) − (A)
④ (C) − (A) − (B)　　⑤ (C) − (B) − (A)

**⊕ 다이어트에 대한 경고**
미국 영양사 협회에서는 체중 조절을 위한 획기적인 식품이나 음식은 지구상에 없으며, 일부 식품군의 섭취를 엄격히 제한하게 되면 체중 감량이 아닌, 영양 불균형을 초래하며, 다이어트 식품을 사는 행위는 체중을 줄이는 것이 아니라 지갑 무게만 줄인다고 경고했다.

New Words

| | | | | | |
|---|---|---|---|---|---|
| ☐ deficit | 부족 | ☐ combination | 조합 | ☐ maximize | 최대화하다 |
| ☐ promote | 촉진하다 | ☐ strategic | 전략적인 | ☐ metabolism | 신진대사 |
| ☐ effect | 효과 | ☐ interval | 간격 | ☐ significantly | 상당히 |
| ☐ body composition | (신)체성분 | ☐ protein | 단백질 | ☐ intake | 섭취 |
| ☐ muscle mass | 근육량 | ☐ carbohydrates | 탄수화물 | ☐ deliver | 전달하다 |

# 02

**다음 글의 내용과 일치하지 <u>않는</u> 것은?**

56% 고2 06월 모의고사 지문/문제 변형

The world can be a different and better place if, while you are here, you give of yourself. This concept became clear to Azim one day when he watched television at an airport terminal while he was waiting for a flight. A priest was sharing a story about newborn twins, and one of them was ill. The twins were in separate incubators, as per hospital rules. A nurse on the floor repeatedly suggested that the twins be kept together in one incubator. The doctors finally agreed to try putting together in the same place. When the twins were able to touch each other, the healthy twin immediately put his arms around his sick brother. This instinctive connection little by little helped the sick twin to recover and to regain his health. The babies' family and the doctors witnessed the intangible force of love and the incredible power of giving.

*intangible 만질 수 없는

① 갓 태어난 쌍둥이 중에 한 명이 아팠다.
② 쌍둥이들은 병원 규칙대로 공유된 인큐베이터에 있었다.
③ 간호사는 쌍둥이들이 인큐베이터에 함께 있어야 한다고 제안했다.
④ 인큐베이터에서 건강한 쌍둥이가 아픈 남동생을 자신의 팔로 감쌌다.
⑤ 쌍둥이들의 본능적인 교감으로 아픈 쌍둥이의 건강은 회복되었다.

**➕ 캥거루 케어(Kangaroo care)**
엄마와 아기가 서로 피부를 맞대고 안고 있는 것으로 1983년 인큐베이터의 부족으로 캥거루처럼 엄마 품속에서 아기를 돌보면서 시작되었다. 실제로 호주에서 6개월 만에 태어난 아이가 사망선고를 받자 엄마는 본능적으로 아기의 체온을 유지하는 캥거루 케어를 했고 의료진도 포기한 생명을 살렸다.

New Words

| | | | | | |
|---|---|---|---|---|---|
| □ give of | 헌신하다 | □ separate | 분리된 | □ recover | 회복하다 |
| □ concept | 생각, 개념 | □ as per | ~에 따라 | □ regain | 되찾다 |
| □ clear | 명확한 | □ immediately | 즉시 | □ witness | 목격하다 |
| □ priest | 성직자 | □ instinctive | 본능적인 | □ force | 힘 |
| □ newborn | 갓 태어난 | □ little by little | 조금씩, 점차적으로 | □ incredible | 믿을 수 없는 |

## 03

71% 고3 07월 모의고사 변형

밑줄 친 **a premature baby in an incubator**가 다음 글에서 의미하는 바로 가장 적절한 것은?

Consider the world as <u>a premature baby in an incubator</u>. The baby's health status is extremely bad and her breathing, heart rate, and other important signs are tracked constantly in order that changes for better or worse can quickly be confirmed. After a week, she is getting much better. On all the main measures, she is improving, but she still has to stay in the incubator since her health is still at stake. Does it make sense to say that the infant's situation is improving? Yes. Absolutely. Does it make sense to say it is bad? Yes. Absolutely. Does saying "things are improving" imply that everything is fine, and we should all relax and not worry? No, not at all. Is it valuable to have to choose between bad and improving? Definitely not. It's both. That is the way we must think about the current state of the world.

① happening too early when no one is ready for it
② being expected to grow up and face a bright future
③ lacking essential competence, not functioning properly
④ being in a dangerous situation with no hope to improve
⑤ having signs of getting better, but still not in good condition

➕ 신생아 특징과 발달
출생 후 1일부터 30일까지의 갓 태어난 아기를 신생아라고 칭한다. 보통 키가 50cm 전후, 몸무게는 평균 3.3kg으로 생후 일주일이 지나면 작은 목소리에도 반응한다. 오감 중 시각이 가장 늦게 발달한다. 기본적으로 시각 운동, 언어, 운동신경, 사회성, 적응성의 다섯 가지 항목을 통해 신생아의 발달을 평가한다.

New Words

| | | | | | |
|---|---|---|---|---|---|
| □ premature | 미숙아 | □ track | 추적하다 | □ infant | 아기, 유아 |
| □ status | 상태, 지위 | □ confirm | 확인하다 | □ Absolutely. | 물론이다. |
| □ breathing | 호흡 | □ measure | 척도 | □ imply | 암시하다, 추론하다 |
| □ heart rate | 심장박동 수 | □ at stake | 위태로운 | □ valuable | 가치가 있는 |
| □ sign | 징후 | □ make sense | 이치에 맞다 | □ definitely | 절대로, 분명히 |

**01** 다음 주어진 단어를 활용하여 빈칸을 완성하시오.

| cease | deficit | strategic | instinctive | status |

(1) Finally the snow has _____ .

(2) Korea is on the verge of a budget _____ .

(3) It is time for us to make a _____ retreat.

(4) After he confirmed my _____ reaction, he noticed my thoughts.

(5) Most people spend their entire lives trying to improve their social _____ .

**02** 다음 영영풀이에 해당하는 단어를 보기에서 골라 쓰시오.

보기
| ethical | absence | modification | promote | deliver |
| give of | separate | witness | at stake | imply |

(1) _____ : at issue or at risk

(2) _____ : morally good or correct

(3) _____ : not joined or touching physically

(4) _____ : to see, be present at, or know firsthand

(5) _____ : an alteration or adjustment to something

(6) _____ : to suggest or indicate something indirectly

(7) _____ : the state of not being at a particular place

(8) _____ : to raise to a more important position or rank

(9) _____ : to bring or transport something to its destination

(10) _____ : to contribute something, typically money towards a cause

# MINI TEST

## 01

**다음 글의 주제로 가장 적절한 것은?**

76% 고2 06월 모의고사 변형

A child whose behavior is not controlled improves when clear restrictions on their behavior are established and imposed. However, parents must agree on where a limit will be set and how it will be imposed. The limit and the consequence of breaking the limit must be clearly presented to the child. Enforcement of the limit should be consistent and firm. Too many limits are difficult to learn and may spoil the normal development of autonomy. The limit must be reasonable in terms of the child's age, temperament, and developmental level. To be effective, both parents (and other adults in the home) have to enforce limits. Otherwise, children may effectively split the parents and seek to test the limits with the more indulgent parent. In all situations, to be effective, punishment must be brief and linked directly to a behavior. More effective behavioral change occurs when punishment is also linked to praise of the intended behavior.

\*autonomy 자율성 \*\*indulgent 멋대로 하게 하는

① ways of giving reward and punishment fairly
② considerations when placing limits on children's behavior
③ reasons for encouraging children to do socially right things
④ the increasing necessity of parents' participation in discipline
⑤ the impact of caregivers' personality on children's development

## 02 다음 글의 제목으로 가장 적절한 것은?

86% 고2 09월 모의고사 변형

Since the early 1980s, Black Friday has been a sort of unofficial U.S. holiday marking the beginning of the holiday season and, as a result, the most profitable time in the year for retailers. But in recent years, a new movement has come to light, adding a more ecological philosophy. The movement is called Green Friday, and it seeks to raise awareness about the damage which Black Friday brings to the environment. Think of the carbon emissions which are caused by driving to the mall, and even the long-term waste which is produced by mindlessly buying things that we don't need. Green Friday is about changing the way we see this day and switching our mindset from "buy, buy, buy" to finding alternative ways to give gifts during the holiday season so we don't cause further damage to the Earth. Even if only a small percentage of the population makes the switch, it'll mean great things for the environment.

① Turning Black Friday Green
② Compare Deals, Save Money
③ Online Shops for Green Consumers
④ Marketing Tricks Used on Black Friday
⑤ What Makes You Spend Beyond Your Budget?

## 03

다음 글의 밑줄 친 부분 중, 어법상 틀린 것은?  `35%` 고2 09월 모의고사 변형

Humans are not only ① <u>unique</u> in the sense that they began to use an ever-widening tool set, but we are also the only species on this planet that has constructed forms of complexity which use external energy sources. This was a fundamental new development, ② <u>which</u> there were no precedents in history. This capacity may first have emerged between 1.5 and 0.5 million years ago, when humans began to control fire. From at least 50,000 years ago, some of the energy which was stored in air and water flows ③ <u>was used</u> for navigation and, much later, also for powering the first machines. Around 10,000 years ago, humans learned to cultivate plants and ④ <u>tame</u> animals and thus control these significant matter and energy flows. Very soon, they also learned to use animal muscle power. About 250 years ago, fossil fuels began to be used on a large scale for powering machines of many different kinds, thereby ⑤ <u>creating</u> the virtually unlimited amounts of artificial complexity that we are familiar with today.

\*precedent 전례

## 04

다음 글의 밑줄 친 부분 중, 문맥상 낱말의 쓰임이 적절하지 <u>않은</u> 것은?  `47%` 고2 06월 모의고사 변형

Allowing people to influence each other reduces the ① <u>precision</u> of a group's estimate. In order to derive the most useful information from multiple sources of evidence, you should always try to make these sources ② <u>independent</u> of each other. This rule is part of good police procedure. When there are multiple witnesses to an event, they are not allowed to ③ <u>discuss</u> it before giving their testimony. The goal is not just to prevent collusion by hostile witnesses, but to prohibit witnesses from influencing each other as well. Witnesses who exchange their experiences will tend to make similar errors in their testimony, ④ <u>improving</u> the total value of the information that they provide. The standard practice of ⑤ <u>open</u> discussion gives too much weight to the opinions of those who speak early and confidently and it causes others to line up behind them.

\*testimony 증언  \*\*collusion 공모, 담합

## 05 다음 빈칸에 들어갈 말로 가장 적절한 것은?

47% 고2 11월 모의고사 변형

In the modern world, we look for certainty in uncertain places. We search for order in chaos, the right answer in ambiguity, and conviction in complexity. "We spend much more time and effort on trying to control the world," best-selling writer Yuval Noah Harari says, "than on trying to understand it." We look for the easy-to-follow formula. Over time, _____. Our approach reminds me of the classic story of the drunk man searching for his keys under a street lamp at night. He knows that he lost his keys somewhere on the dark side of the street but looks for them underneath the lamp, because that's where the light is. Our yearning for certainty leads us to pursue seemingly safe solutions — by looking for our keys under street lamps. In place of taking a risky walk into the dark, we stay within our current state, no matter how inferior it may be.

① weigh the pros and cons of our actions
② develop the patience to bear ambiguity
③ enjoy adventure rather than settle down
④ gain insight from solving complex problems
⑤ lose our ability to interact with the unknown

# 06

**주어진 글 다음에 이어질 글의 순서로 가장 적절한 것은?**    [53%] 고2 04월 모의고사 변형

Habits create the foundation for mastery. In chess, it is only after the basic movements of the pieces have become automatic that a player can focus on the next level of the game. Each chunk of information which is memorized opens up the mental space for more effortful thinking.

(A) You fall into mindless repetition. It becomes easier to let mistakes slide. When you can do it "good enough" automatically, you stop thinking about how you should do it better.

(B) However, the benefits of habits come at a cost. To begin with, each repetition develops fluency, speed, and skill. But then, while a habit becomes automatic, you become less sensitive to feedback.

(C) This is true for anything that you attempt. When you know the simple movements so well that you are able to perform them without thinking, you are free to pay attention to more advanced details. In this way, habits are the backbone of any pursuit of excellence.

① (A) – (C) – (B)        ② (B) – (A) – (C)        ③ (B) – (C) – (A)
④ (C) – (A) – (B)        ⑤ (C) – (B) – (A)

## 07

글의 흐름으로 보아, 주어진 문장이 들어가기에 가장 적절한 곳은?   55% 고2 03월 모의고사 변형

> Meanwhile, if you are setting some money aside for auto repairs and pay down your debt a little slower, you will feel satisfied that you planned for the auto repair.

If you spend all your extra money reducing debt without saving for the things that are likely to happen, you will feel desperate when something does happen. You will end up going further into debt. ( ① ) Let's suppose you unexpectedly need $500 to have your car repaired. ( ② ) If you don't save for this, you'll end up having another debt. ( ③ ) You'll feel frustrated that you have been trying so hard to pay things off and yet nothing changed. ( ④ ) You will have cash to pay for it, and you are still paying down your debt on schedule. ( ⑤ ) Instead of frustration and disappointment from the unexpected auto repair, you will feel proud and content.

## 08

다음 글에서 전체 흐름과 관계 없는 문장은?   54% 고2 06월 모의고사 변형

People often take it for granted that if a Hadza adult of Tanzania does not know how to solve an algebraic equation, then he must be less intelligent than we are. ① Yet there is no evidence that people from some cultures are fast learners and people from others are slow learners. ② According to a study of comparative cultures, people in different cultures learn different cultural content (attitudes, values, ideas, and behavioral patterns) and they accomplish this with similar efficiency. ③ The traditional Hadza hunter has not learned algebra because such knowledge would not particularly help with his adaptation to life in the East African grasslands. ④ Consequently, he failed to adjust to the environment of the grasslands because he was short of survival skills. ⑤ However, he does know how to trace a wounded bush buck that he has not seen for three days and where to find groundwater.

*algebraic equation 대수 방정식  **bush buck 부시벅(아프리카 영양)  ***comparative culture 비교문화

## 01

밑줄 친 insert "complete" instead of "perfect"가 다음 글에서 의미하는 바로 가장 적절한 것은?

48% 고2 06월 모의고사 변형

You can be perfect, but you need another perspective of being perfect. Perfection actually is possible if you insert "complete" instead of "perfect." Imagine a basketball player taking a fifteen-foot shot and the ball going through the net, never touching the rim. Someone is likely to acclaim, "That was a perfect shot!" And it was perfect. The perfect shot gives his team two points. Now again imagine that same player taking another fifteen-foot shot. But this time the ball hits one side of the rim, rolls around and stands still for half a second, then finally falls through the net. People might be disappointed that it was not a "perfect" shot, and they would be right. But basketball games are not about such criteria as pretty or ugly. Just as the former "perfect" shot, the ball went through the net and the scoreboard increased by two points. In this light, the second shot was as perfect as the first.

*rim 가장자리

① redefine perfection based on task accomplishment
② distinguish what you can achieve from what you can't
③ make something free of flaws to be absolutely perfect
④ take a social perspective on what you have completed
⑤ complete the small stuff first to deal with the big stuff

## 02

다음 글의 주제로 가장 적절한 것은?

48% 고2 06월 모의고사 변형

How can we acquire the nutrients we need with the environment less damaged? It is livestock, the most significant component of agriculture, that contributes most to climate change. Globally, beef cattle and milk cattle have the most significant impact in terms of greenhouse gas emissions(GHGEs), and account for 41% of the world's $CO_2$ emissions and 20% of the total global GHGEs. There are other causes that increase the amount of GHGEs in the atmosphere. The transport, land clearance, methane emissions, and grain cultivation also associated with the livestock industry are the main drivers behind increases in global temperatures. In contrast to conventional livestock, insects "mini livestock" emit less GHGEs, use minimal land, can live on food waste rather than cultivated grain, and can be raised anywhere, potentially avoiding GHGEs caused by long distance transportation. If we encouraged insect consumption and refrained from meat consumption worldwide, the chance of global warming that the food system causes would be substantially reduced.

① ways of productivity enhancement in agriculture
② effects of supply and demand on farming insects
③ importance of reducing greenhouse gas emissions
④ technological advances to prevent global warming
⑤ necessity of a dietary shift toward eating insects

## 03

**다음 글의 제목으로 가장 적절한 것은?**  51% 고2 06월 모의고사 변형

We associate our image of the world with what most easily comes to mind. This is absurd, of course, because in reality, what we can easily recall has nothing to do with how frequently things happen. Due to this prejudice, it is likely that we travel through life with an incorrect risk map in our heads. Thus, there is a fear of us being the victims of a plane crash, car accident, or a murder, and we overlook the risk of dying from less noticeable means, such as diabetes or stomach cancer. The chances of bomb attacks are much rarer than we think, and those of suffering depression are much higher. We are obsessed with the likelihood of spectacular, flashy, or loud outcomes. Anything silent or invisible we belittle in our minds. Our brains imagine extreme outcomes more easily than ordinary ones.

*diabetes 당뇨병 **flashy 현란한 ***belittle 무시하다

① We Weigh Dramatic Things More!
② Brains Think Logically, Not Emotionally
③ Our Brains' Preference for Positive Images
④ How Can People Overcome Their Prejudices?
⑤ The Way to Reduce Errors in Risk Analysis

## 04

**다음 글의 밑줄 친 부분 중, 어법상 틀린 것은?**  48% 고2 09월 모의고사 변형

Whether cats are liquid or solid is the kind of question that could earn a scientist an Ig Nobel Prize that honors research that "makes people laugh, then think", which is a parody of the Nobel Prize. But this question wasn't what was in mind first ① when Marc-Antoine Fardin, a physicist at Paris Diderot University, set out to find out whether house cats flow. Fardin noticed that these furry pets can adjust to the shape of the container they sit in ② similar to what fluids do. So he applied rheology, the branch of physics that handles the deformation of matter, to calculate the time ③ it takes for cats to settle down in the space of a vase or bathroom sink. The conclusion? Cats can be either liquid or solid, depending on the circumstances. A cat in a tiny box will behave like a fluid, ④ filling up all the space. But a cat in a bathtub will try to prevent water from reaching it and ⑤ behave very much like a solid

*rheology 유동학 **deformation 변형

## 05

다음 글의 밑줄 친 부분 중, 문맥상 낱말의 쓰임이 적절하지 <u>않은</u> 것은? 50% 고2 06월 모의고사 변형

Sudden success can be very dangerous. In terms of Neurology, this causes some chemicals giving a powerful burst of excitement and energy to be released in the brain, which leads to the desire to ① <u>repeat</u> this experience. Some kinds of addictions or manic behavior could result. Also, when gains come quickly, we tend to ② <u>lose</u> sight of the basic wisdom that true success must come through hard work. We do not realize the role that luck plays in such ③ <u>hard-earned</u> gains. We try to recapture that delight from winning a lot of money or attention. We acquire feelings of superiority and become especially ④ <u>resistant</u> to anyone who tries to warn us, saying they are jealous. Because this cannot be sustained, we experience an inevitable ⑤ <u>fall</u>, which is much more painful, leading to the depression part of the cycle.

## 06

다음 빈칸에 들어갈 말로 가장 적절한 것은? 70% 고2 03월 모의고사 변형

Nothing happens immediately, so we can't see any results at first. A man tries to make a fire by rubbing two sticks of wood together. He says to himself, "I can make a fire with this wood," and he begins rubbing with all his effort. He rubs on and on, but he's not very patient. So he gets discouraged and stops to rest for a while. He starts again, but then rests again. By then the heat has disappeared, since he didn't continue for long enough. Ultimately, he stops altogether. He becomes more and more discouraged until he gives up completely, saying "There's no fire here." Actually, he was doing the work, but there wasn't enough heat to start a fire. The fire was there all the time, but _____.

① he didn't carry on to the end
② someone told him not to give up
③ the sticks were not strong enough
④ he started without planning in advance
⑤ the weather was not suitable to start a fire

# 07

**주어진 글 다음에 이어질 글의 순서로 가장 적절한 것은?**

[77%] 고2 09월 모의고사 변형

> When a change occurs in the environment, a relative increase or decrease works in the rate at which the neurons fire. Intensity is coded and relativity operates to control our sensations.

(A) Even though both hands are now in the same water, one feels that it is colder and the other warmer because of the relative change from prior experience. This process is called adaptation.

(B) For example, place one hand in hot water and the other in iced water before both hands are put into lukewarm water. You will experience conflicting sensations of temperature.

(C) It explains why you get blind inside a dark room once you have come in from a sunny day. Your eyes have to become accustomed to the new level of intensity of light. It also explains the reason apples taste sour after eating sweet chocolate.

*lukewarm 미지근한

① (A) – (C) – (B)　　　② (B) – (A) – (C)　　　③ (B) – (C) – (A)

④ (C) – (A) – (B)　　　⑤ (C) – (B) – (A)

## 08 글의 흐름으로 보아, 주어진 문장이 들어가기에 가장 적절한 곳은?

49% 고2 03월 모의고사 변형

> Rather, it is the air moving through a small hole into a closed container, as a result of air being blown out of the container by a fan inside.

Hubert Cecil Booth is often credited with inventing the first powered mobile vacuum cleaner. ( ① ) Actually, he only claimed to be the first to coin the term "vacuum cleaner." ( ② ) The term "vacuum" used for this device is an inappropriate name, because there is no vacuum in a vacuum cleaner. ( ③ ) But the "rapid air movement in a closed container to create suction" cleaner would not sound as scientific. ( ④ ) Anyway, we have used the "vacuum" since its invention, and it is hard to find any references to "vacuum" prior to Booth. ( ⑤ ) Interestingly, Booth himself did not mention the term "vacuum" when he filed a provisional specification describing his intended invention.

*coin (신조어를) 만들다 **provisional specification 임시 제품 설명서

# 01 다음 글의 주제로 가장 적절한 것은?

**64%** 고2 03월 모의고사 변형

Recreation may take a variety of forms and it also meets a wide range of individual needs and interests. Many participants take part in recreation as a form of relaxation and release from work pressures or other tensions. Typically, they may be passive spectators of entertainment who enjoy television, movies, or other forms of electronic amusement. However, other significant play motivations are based on the need to express creativity, discover hidden talents, or pursue excellence in various forms of personal expression. For some participants, active and competitive recreation may offer the opportunity to release hostility and aggression. It sometimes helps them struggle against others or the environment in adventurous, high-risk activities. Others participate in recreation that is highly social and provides the opportunity for making new friends or cooperating with others in group settings.

① effects of recreational participation on memory
② importance of balance between work and leisure
③ various motivations for recreational participation
④ social factors promoting the recreation movement
⑤ economic trends affecting recreational participation

## 02

**다음 글의 제목으로 가장 적절한 것은?**

76% 고2 06월 모의고사 변형

Many inventions were created thousands of years ago, so it can be difficult to know their exact origins. From time to time scientists discover a model of an early invention. From this model they can accurately tell us how old it is and where it came from. However, there is always the possibility that other scientists will discover even older models of the same invention in a different part of the world, too. The invention of pottery is a good example. For many years archaeologists believed pottery was first invented in the Near East (around modern Iran). They supposed that it dated back to 9,000 B.C. In the 1960s, however, older pots from 10,000 B.C. were found in another country. There is always a possibility that archaeologists will find even older pots somewhere else in the future.

① How Can You Tell Original from Fake?
② Exploring the Materials of Ancient Pottery
③ Origin of Inventions: Never-ending Journey
④ Learn from the Past, Change for the Better
⑤ Science as a Driving Force for Human Civilization

## 03

**다음 글의 밑줄 친 부분 중, 어법상 틀린 것은?**

50% 고2 1월 모의고사 변형

The spotlight effect is the phenomenon by which we see ourselves at center stage, thus naturally overestimating the extent ① to which others pay attention to us. Timothy Lawson researched the spotlight effect by having college students ② change into a sweatshirt with a big popular logo on the front before meeting a group of peers. Nearly 40 percent of them ③ were sure the other students would remember what was on the shirt, but only 10 percent actually did. Most observers did not even notice ④ that the students changed sweatshirts after leaving the room for a few minutes. In another experiment, even noticeable clothes, such as a T-shirt with singer Barry Manilow on it, ⑤ provoking only 23 percent of observers to notice — far fewer than the 50 percent estimated by the students who were wearing the T-shirt.

## 04

다음 글의 밑줄 친 부분 중, 문맥상 낱말의 쓰임이 적절하지 <u>않은</u> 것은? 39% 고2 09월 모의고사 변형

Although he was an advocate of free speech and religious toleration, Voltaire created a lot of controversy. For example, he declared, "I hate what you say, but will defend your right to say it." That was a powerful ① <u>defense</u> of the idea that any trivial opinion deserves to be heard. However, the Catholic Church strictly ② <u>controlled</u> what could be published. Many of Voltaire's books were censored and burned publicly, and he was even imprisoned for ③ <u>insulting</u> noblemen. But none of this stopped him from challenging the prejudices and pretensions of those around him. In one of his philosophical novels, he completely ④ <u>supported</u> the contemporary religious optimism about humanity and the universe in an interesting way, making the book a bestseller. Wisely, Voltaire left his name ⑤ <u>off</u> the book, otherwise he would have been imprisoned again for making fun of religious beliefs.

*pretension 가식

## 05

다음 빈칸에 들어갈 말로 가장 적절한 것은? 53% 고2 05월 예비 모의고사 변형

It has long been suggested that if you postpone your ideas and decisions, they may well improve. It is obviously true that to put off making a decision is itself a decision. The political process is essentially a system of delay and deliberation. So, for that matter, is the creation of a great painting, a book, or a building like Blenheim Palace, which took the Duke of Marlborough's architects and laborers 15 years to construct. In the process, the design can be softened and enriched. Indeed, _____ can be the obstacle to elegance. As T.H. White, author of *Sword in the Stone*, once wrote, time "is not meant to be spent in an hour or a day, but consumed carefully and gradually and without hurry." In other words, what you don't necessarily have to do today, put off until tomorrow.

*deliberation 협의

① hurry                  ② caution                  ③ complexity
④ imitation              ⑤ system

# 06 주어진 글 다음에 이어질 글의 순서로 가장 적절한 것은?

Like the physiological discoveries of the late nineteenth century, today's biological breakthrough has radically changed our understanding of how the human organism works and will change medical practice completely and fundamentally.

(A) Do you remember the scientific method you first learned about when in elementary school? It has a long and difficult process of observation, hypothesis, experiment, testing, modifying, retesting, and retesting again and again.

(B) That's how science works. The breakthrough understanding of the relationship between our genes and chronic disease happened in that way, based on the work of scientists from the past. In fact, it is still happening; the story continues to evolve as the research goes on.

(C) In many people's minds, the word "breakthrough" seems to mean an amazing, novel discovery that instantly makes everything clear. However, science doesn't actually work that way.

*chronic 만성적인

① (A) – (C) – (B)      ② (B) – (A) – (C)      ③ (B) – (C) – (A)
④ (C) – (A) – (B)      ⑤ (C) – (B) – (A)

# 07 글의 흐름으로 보아, 주어진 문장이 들어가기에 가장 적절한 곳은?

47% 고2 09월 모의고사 변형

> This allows the solids to carry the waves more easily and efficiently, producing a louder sound.

Tap the surface of a wooden table with your finger, and observe the loudness of the sound you hear. Then, place your ear close to top of the table. ( ① ) With your finger about one foot away from your ear, tap the table top and observe the loudness again. ( ② ) The sound you hear with your ear on the desk is much louder than that off the desk. ( ③ ) Sound waves can travel through many solid materials as well as through the air. ( ④ ) Solids, like wood, transfer the sound waves much better than air because the molecules in solids are much closer and more concentrated than those in the air. ( ⑤ ) The density of the air itself also plays a determining factor in the loudness of the sound waves passing through it.

\*molecule 분자

정답과 해설 p.42

08

43% 고2 06월 모의고사 변형

**다음 글의 내용을 한 문장으로 요약하고자 한다. 빈칸 (A)와 (B)에 들어갈 말로 가장 적절한 것은?**

The self is formed by social environment, by looking outwards as well as inwards. Leon Festinger's theory describes how other people shape who you are. For example, imagine that you feel like you're good at math because you were the top student in your class. But you think that you're bad at dancing after seeing other people dance at the school festival. These facts are neither objective nor fixed, of course. If you happen to be placed in a classroom of future mathematicians, without doubt you feel that you're relatively bad at math. Looking on the bright side, however, you may feel like you're better at dancing. Festinger realized that these social comparisons aren't entirely accidental. Humans actively seek out particular people and select particular skills or aspects for comparison.

↓

> People ____(A)____ a sense of who they are by ____(B)____ themselves against those around them.

|  | (A) | (B) |  | (A) | (B) |
|---|---|---|---|---|---|
| ① | achieve | ...... defending | ② | acquire | ...... weighing |
| ③ | forget | ...... evaluating | ④ | ignore | ...... competing |
| ⑤ | overestimate | ...... disregarding |  |  |  |

MEMO

수능 영어를 향한 가벼운 발걸음

# 맨 처음 수능 영어

## 주제별 독해

**Workbook** **2**

다락원

| Q | •••••••••••••••••••••••••••••••••••••••••••••••••••••• | 주제별 연습 01 | ••••••••••••••••••••••••••••

**A 우리말은 영어로, 영어는 우리말로 쓰시오.**

1 earn _____

2 degree _____

3 advancement _____

4 장소, 현장 _____

5 보존하다, 보호하다 _____

6 정치적인 _____

**B 괄호 안의 주어진 단어를 바르게 배열하시오.**

1 She helped (some of Turkey's, preserve, most important, archaeological sites).

→ _____

2 Her work (won, Turkey's cultural heritage, her, a Prince Claus Award, preserving).

→ _____

**C 다음 빈칸에 들어갈 알맞은 단어를 적으시오.**

1 그녀는 비밀들을 드러냈을 뿐만 아니라, 자신의 시대의 분위기를 다루었다.

She _____ _____ the _____ of her time _____ _____ _____ revealed the secrets.

2 그녀는 그것을 발견함으로써 인류의 가장 오래된 것으로 알려진 문명 중 하나를 발굴했다.

She _____ _____ one of humanity's oldest known _____ _____ _____ it.

**D 다음 괄호 안의 주어진 단어를 활용하여 문장을 완성하시오.**

1 Cambel은 그 경기에 출전한 최초의 무슬림 여성이 되었다. (Muslim woman, compete, the Games) 11단어

→ _____
_____

2 그녀는 Adolf Hitler를 만나도록 초대를 받았지만 정치적인 이유로 그것을 거절했다. (invite, meet, reject, on, reasons) 13단어

→ _____
_____

**A 우리말은 영어로, 영어는 우리말로 쓰시오.**

1 individual _____

2 break free _____

3 turn to _____

4 지나가다 _____

5 잡다, 쥐다 _____

6 제안하다, 시사하다 _____

**B 괄호 안의 주어진 단어를 바르게 배열하시오.**

1 He asked (to, why, try, the beast, didn't, away, get).

→ _____

2 He suggested to his son (should, the question to, that, the trainer, he, ask).

→ _____

**C 다음 빈칸에 들어갈 알맞은 단어를 적으시오.**

1 그가 아무리 열심히 대답을 생각해 내려고 해도, 그는 줄 수 있는 좋은 대답이 없었다.

_____ _____ _____ _____ he tried to think of an answer, he didn't have a good one to give.

2 그는 코끼리를 제외한 동물들을 보러 가기로 결심했는데, 그것은 밧줄에 묶여 있었다.

He _____ to see the animals _____ _____ the elephant, _____ was _____ with a rope.

**D 다음 괄호 안의 주어진 단어를 활용하여 문장을 완성하시오.**

1 그는 단순히 밧줄을 삶의 방식으로 받아들였다. (simply accept, the, a way of life) 10단어

→ _____
_____

2 비록 이 코끼리가 크고 힘이 센 것 같지만, 그는 밧줄을 걷어차고 도망갈 수 없다. (Although, look, huge and strong, kick, and run away) 15단어

→ _____
_____

## 주제별 연습 02

**A 우리말은 영어로, 영어는 우리말로 쓰시오.**

1 blame   _____

2 confidence   _____

3 take a risk   _____

4 건네다; 손   _____

5 겁에 질린, 무서워하는   _____

6 내용(물); 만족하는   _____

**B 괄호 안의 주어진 단어를 바르게 배열하시오.**

1 Alexander (that, him, completely trusted, him, he, told).

  → _____

2 (down, terrified, he, Extremely, threw, himself) at the king's bedside.

  → _____

**C 다음 빈칸에 들어갈 알맞은 단어를 적으시오.**

1 왕은 자신의 군대 앞에 다시 나타날 수 있을 만큼 충분히 회복되었다.

  The king was well _____ _____ _____ again before his army.

2 의사들은 그를 치료하는 것을 두려워했지만, Philip은 기꺼이 위험을 감수했다.

  Although physicians _____ _____ _____ treat him, Philip _____ _____ _____ take the risk.

**D 다음 괄호 안의 주어진 단어를 활용하여 문장을 완성하시오.**

1 Alexander는 누구에게도 보여주지 않고서 그 편지를 읽었다. (without, show, to anyone) 9단어

  → _____

2 Alexander는 그 의사가 그를 독살하도록 뇌물을 받았다고 쓰여 있는 편지를 받았다. (receive, say that, the physician, had, bribe, poison) 14단어

  → _____

## 주제별 연습 03

**A 우리말은 영어로, 영어는 우리말로 쓰시오.**

1 flaw   _____

2 flightless   _____

3 rate   _____

4 경쟁하다   _____

5 먹어치우다   _____

6 즉각, 즉시   _____

**B 괄호 안의 주어진 단어를 바르게 배열하시오.**

1 This destruction (a fast growing industry, was, by, the needs of, caused).

  → _____

2 (one, There, direct reason, was, that) the local people were cutting down the reeds.

  → _____

**C 다음 빈칸에 들어갈 알맞은 단어를 적으시오.**

1 Atitlán 호수에 약 80마리만이 남겨져 있었다.

  _____ _____ only around 80 birds _____ on Lake Atitlán.

2 한 항공사가 그 호수를 관광지로 개발하는 데 관심을 보였다.

  An airline _____ _____ _____ developing the lake _____ a tourist destination.

**D 다음 괄호 안의 주어진 단어를 활용하여 문장을 완성하시오.**

1 특별히 선택된 물고기 종이 도입되었다. (A specially, select, species of fish, introduce) 8단어

  → _____

2 그 호수에는 어떤 적절한 스포츠용(낚시용) 물고기도 없었다. (lack, any, suitable, sporting fish) 7단어

  → _____

| Q | ⋯⋯⋯⋯⋯⋯⋯⋯⋯⋯ | 주제별 연습 01 | ⋯⋯⋯⋯⋯⋯

**A** 우리말은 영어로, 영어는 우리말로 쓰시오.

1 benefit _____

2 maximize _____

3 economist _____

4 추구 _____

5 협업 _____

6 경쟁 _____

**B** 괄호 안의 주어진 단어를 바르게 배열하시오.

1 He described the pursuit of (guides, self-interest as, the economy, qualities, that).

→ _____

2 When parties work together, (almost, expands, always, size of, the overall, benefit).

→ _____

**C** 다음 빈칸에 들어갈 알맞은 단어를 적으시오.

1 똑똑한 경쟁자들은 그들이 할 수 있을 때마다 협력한다.
Smart competitors _____ _____ they _____.

2 경쟁적인 사람들은 그의 철학을 수학자의 생각으로 대체하고 있다.
Competitive people are _____ his philosophy _____ the thinking of the _____.

**D** 다음 괄호 안의 주어진 단어를 활용하여 문장을 완성하시오.

1 그들이 홀로 행동할 때, 네 명의 사냥꾼은 각각 한 마리의 토끼만 잡을 수 있다. (Four, only, each when, act) 12단어

→ _____
_____

2 협력하는 환경의 사람들이 전통적인 환경의 사람들보다 업무 수행을 더 잘 한다. (People, in, environments, perform, those, in traditional) 11단어

→ _____
_____

**A** 우리말은 영어로, 영어는 우리말로 쓰시오.

1 argue _____

2 weigh _____

3 judgement _____

4 관찰하다 _____

5 흉내 내다 _____

6 무의식적인 _____

**B** 괄호 안의 주어진 단어를 바르게 배열하시오.

1 Philosophers have long argued (people, one, understand, about, how, another).

→ _____

2 People test explanations, giving (scientists, rational, the impression, they are, that).

→ _____

**C** 다음 빈칸에 들어갈 알맞은 단어를 적으시오.

1 우리는 그것들을 시시각각으로 우리가 관찰하는 증거에 반하여 검증한다.
We test them _____ the evidence we observe _____ by _____.

2 우리는 다른 사람들이 어떻게 행동할 것인지에 대한 가설을 생각해 낸다.
We _____ _____ _____ _____ about _____ other people will _____.

**D** 다음 괄호 안의 주어진 단어를 활용하여 문장을 완성하시오.

1 이러한 종류의 가설 검증이 우리가 서로를 이해하는 방법의 일부이다. (This sort, testing, part of, how, one another) 13단어

→ _____
_____

2 우리는 그들이 경험하고 있는 것을 느낌으로써 다른 사람들이 느끼는 것을 이해한다. (what, others, by, experience) 11단어

→ _____
_____

**A** 우리말은 영어로, 영어는 우리말로 쓰시오.

1 fragility _____

2 intimate _____

3 unstable _____

4 상황 _____

5 동반자 _____

6 주목할 만한 _____

**B** 괄호 안의 주어진 단어를 바르게 배열하시오.

1 The life of the bowl is (under, dangerous, always, circumstances).

→ _____

2 We love the cast of twilight across (only, lasting, a moment, a mountainside).

→ _____

**C** 다음 빈칸에 들어갈 알맞은 단어를 적으시오.

1 그의 말은 자신의 삶이 죽어가고 있다는 바로 그 사실로 가득 차 있다.

His words are _____ _____ the _____ fact of his own life _____ away.

2 도자기 그릇은 언젠가는 깨질 것이라는 이유로 아름답다.

The china bowl is beautiful _____ _____ _____ _____ it will, someday, break.

**D** 다음 괄호 안의 주어진 단어를 활용하여 문장을 완성하시오.

1 우리는 진짜 꽃을 플라스틱 꽃보다 훨씬 더 사랑한다. (real, so much, one) 12단어

→ _____

_____

2 생명을 소중하게 만드는 것은 삶의 연약함이다. (It, the weakness, that, precious) 10단어

→ _____

_____

**A** 우리말은 영어로, 영어는 우리말로 쓰시오.

1 deny _____

2 gene _____

3 variety _____

4 구현하다 _____

5 종교적인 _____

6 반영하다 _____

**B** 괄호 안의 주어진 단어를 바르게 배열하시오.

1 Thoughts, whether original or conventional, (identified, individuals, are, with).

→ _____

2 (from Plato, by philosophers, Influenced, Descartes, to), it says that they have creativity.

→ _____

**C** 다음 빈칸에 들어갈 알맞은 단어를 적으시오.

1 그들이 하는 특별한 것들은 그들의 유전자와 두뇌에 기인한다.

The special things they do are _____ _____ their _____ and their brains.

2 우리의 개인성은 부인되는 것이 아니라, 특정한 문화적 경험의 산물로 여겨진다.

Our individuality is _____ denied, _____ viewed _____ a _____ of specific _____ experiences.

**D** 다음 괄호 안의 주어진 단어를 활용하여 문장을 완성하시오.

1 뇌 그 자체가 사회적인 것이며, 구조적으로 영향을 받는다. (itself, structurally, influence) 9단어

→ _____

_____

2 문화적인 영향과 원인들은 고려 사항으로부터 완전히 제거된다. (causes, completely, eliminate, consideration) 9단어

→ _____

_____

# UNIT 03 역사, 풍습, 지리

**A** 우리말은 영어로, 영어는 우리말로 쓰시오.

1  contain　　　_____

2  spiritual　　_____

3  socialize　　_____

4  원천　　　　_____

5  효과　　　　_____

6  ~을 전해주다　_____

**B** 괄호 안의 주어진 단어를 바르게 배열하시오.

1  People thought that the power of hair (cause, could, to, exist, the individual).

　→ _____

2  Communication from the gods (the hair, pass through, to, thought to, get to the soul, was).

　→ _____
_____

**C** 다음 빈칸에 들어갈 알맞은 단어를 적으시오.

1  치료 주술사들은 물약을 보호하기 위해 머리카락을 통에 넣었다.

　Medicine men put hair to boxes _____ _____ _____ _____ the potions.

2  많은 아프리카의 문화들은 신체에서 머리를 정체성의 중심이라고 여겼다.

　Many African cultures _____ the head _____ the center of _____ in the body.

**D** 다음 괄호 안의 주어진 단어를 활용하여 문장을 완성하시오.

1  머리카락은 그 자체로 신성한 영혼들과 소통할 수 있는 수단이었다. (Hair itself, a way, communicate, divine spirits) 10단어

　→ _____
_____

2  머리카락이 행운을 가져오거나 악으로부터 지켜줄 수 있다고 여겨졌다. (It, think, that, bring, against evil) 13단어

　→ _____

**A** 우리말은 영어로, 영어는 우리말로 쓰시오.

1  identify　　　_____

2  geographical　_____

3  interconnected　_____

4  회전하다　　　_____

5  내성, 관용　　_____

6  분포, 분배　　_____

**B** 괄호 안의 주어진 단어를 바르게 배열하시오.

1  Their biotas show (those, differences than, evident, on land, fewer).

　→ _____

2  These moving waters (help, to, be, distributed, their young or larvae).

　→ _____

**C** 다음 빈칸에 들어갈 알맞은 단어를 적으시오.

1  지리적 경계들이 대륙의 그것(경계)들보다 식별하기 더 어렵다.

　_____ borders are _____ difficult to _____ _____ _____ of the continents.

2  이 이동하는 해류들은 해양 생물을 여기저기로 운반한다.

　These moving waters carry _____ organisms _____ _____ _____ _____

**D** 다음 괄호 안의 주어진 단어를 활용하여 문장을 완성하시오.

1  방해물이 있을 수 있지만, 탁 트인 대양에 확실한 경계는 없다. (Although, there, may, barriers, no, firm boundaries) 10단어

　→ _____

2  변화도는 다양한 유기체가 서식하는 넓은 지역으로 확장된다. (The gradients, extend over, areas that, a variety of, organisms) 14단어

　→ _____
_____

········| 주제별 연습 02 | ········                              ········| 주제별 연습 03 | ········

**A** 우리말은 영어로, 영어는 우리말로 쓰시오.

1 border _____

2 significant _____

3 foundation _____

4 소(떼) _____

5 거래 _____

6 설명하다 _____

**B** 괄호 안의 주어진 단어를 바르게 배열하시오.

1 The first written documents (simple, transactions using, symbols, record).

→ _____

2 The practice of (was, exchanges for, using clay pieces, to account for) agricultural goods.

→ _____

**C** 다음 빈칸에 들어갈 알맞은 단어를 적으시오.

1 이 변화가 시작된 지역은 비옥한 초승달 지대라고 알려져 있었다.

The region _____ this shift began _____ _____ _____ the Fertile Crescent.

2 수렵과 채집에서 농업에 기초한 정착된 생활 방식으로의 변화가 있었다.

There was a change _____ hunting and _____ _____ a settled lifestyle _____ _____ agriculture.

**D** 다음 괄호 안의 주어진 단어를 활용하여 문장을 완성하시오.

1 쓰기는 작은 점토 조각을 사용하는 관습으로부터 발달했던 것처럼 보인다. (appear, have, evolve, practice of, clay pieces) 13단어

→ _____

_____

2 쓰기의 발달은 시인에 의해서가 아니라, 회계사에 의해 개척되었다. (The development, not by) 11단어

→ _____

_____

**A** 우리말은 영어로, 영어는 우리말로 쓰시오.

1 light _____

2 fertility _____

3 refrain from _____

4 존중하다 _____

5 신화 _____

6 파괴 _____

**B** 괄호 안의 주어진 단어를 바르게 배열하시오.

1 Totems including spiritual rituals (than, objects, are, more).

→ _____

2 This light of the earth (refrain from, causes one, mistreatment of the environment, to).

→ _____

**C** 다음 빈칸에 들어갈 알맞은 단어를 적으시오.

1 원주민들은 환경과 자신들의 관계를 조화로운 연속체로 여긴다.

The aborigines _____ their _____ to the environment _____ a harmonious continuum.

2 그 동기는 부족 신화의 보존과 통합이다

The motivation is the _____ of tribal myths and a(n) _____.

**D** 다음 괄호 안의 주어진 단어를 활용하여 문장을 완성하시오.

1 원주민 문화의 한 가지 놀라운 측면은 토테미즘의 개념이다. (One striking aspect, aboriginal, the concept of totemism) 11단어

→ _____

_____

2 부족의 구성원이 태어날 때 자연 일부의 영혼과 정체성을 취한다. (The tribal member at birth, the soul, a part of nature) 15단어

→ _____

_____

| Q | ·········································· | 주제별 연습 01 | ··········································

## A 우리말은 영어로, 영어는 우리말로 쓰시오.

1  predict  _____

2  observe  _____

3  gravity  _____

4  우주  _____

5  동일한  _____

6  현상  _____

## B 괄호 안의 주어진 단어를 바르게 배열하시오.

1  The field that (may, applies to, different, be, each theory).

→ _____

2  Scientists develop theories to explain (we, what, the universe, observe about).

→ _____

## C 다음 빈칸에 들어갈 알맞은 단어를 적으시오.

1  그 이론들은 현실에 대한 아주 다른 견해를 다룬다.

Those theories _____ _____ very different versions of _____.

2  둘 중 어느 이론도 사과가 떨어지는 것을 설명하는데 사용될 수 있다.

_____ theory can _____ _____ _____ describe the falling of an apple.

## D 다음 괄호 안의 주어진 단어를 활용하여 문장을 완성하시오.

1  Newton은 질량이 힘을 가함으로써 서로에게 영향을 미친다고 생각했다. (imagine, that, masses, apply, a force) 11단어

→ _____

_____

2  Newton의 이론은 당신이 길을 찾는 데 도움이 되는 GPS에 대해 틀린 답을 줄 것이다. (theory, would, the, a GPS, help, navigate) 14단어

→ _____

_____

## A 우리말은 영어로, 영어는 우리말로 쓰시오.

1  scent  _____

2  detect  _____

3  stimulate  _____

4  추론하다  _____

5  떠돌다, 이동하다  _____

6  강화하다  _____

## B 괄호 안의 주어진 단어를 바르게 배열하시오.

1  (There, must, be, that turn, particles of water) into steam.

→ _____

2  The meal (to have, was expecting, I, that) was coming to me in the form of molecules.

→ _____

## C 다음 빈칸에 들어갈 알맞은 단어를 적으시오.

1  고대 그리스인들은 이런 식으로 원자의 개념을 최초로 떠올렸다.

The ancient Greeks first _____ _____ the idea of atoms this way.

2  그것은 원자 이론에 대한 공로를 인정받기에는 너무 늦게 내게 영감을 주었다.

It had _____ me too late to _____ _____ _____ _____ atomic theory.

## D 다음 괄호 안의 주어진 단어를 활용하여 문장을 완성하시오.

1  그 작은 입자들이 너무 작아 보이지 않더라도 그 물은 보존된다. (The water, conserve, even though, particles, too, see) 14단어

→ _____

_____

2  빵 굽는 냄새는 빵의 작은 입자가 눈에 보이지 않게 존재한다는 것을 시사했다. (The smell of baking bread, suggest, that, beyond vision) 14단어

→ _____

_____

**A** 우리말은 영어로, 영어는 우리말로 쓰시오.

1 emit _____

2 breathe _____

3 pollutant _____

4 ~로 이어지다, 야기하다 _____

5 공기, 대기, 분위기 _____

6 적절한, 적당한 _____

**B** 괄호 안의 주어진 단어를 바르게 배열하시오.

1 Carbon dioxide (pollutant, widely, is, to, considered, be, a).

→ _____

2 The need for circulation of air (the control of, is, gases and moisture, related to).

→ _____

**C** 다음 빈칸에 들어갈 알맞은 단어를 적으시오.

1 저장하는 동안 공기 중에 약간의 습기는 탈수를 막아준다.

Some moisture in the air _____ dehydration during _____.

2 온도를 조절하는 것 이외에도 공기의 관리도 중요하다.

_____ _____ temperatures, control of the atmosphere is essential.

**D** 다음 괄호 안의 주어진 단어를 활용하여 문장을 완성하시오.

1 이산화탄소와 습기 양쪽 모두의 수준이 세심하게 조정된다. (The levels, carbon dioxide, modify, carefully) 11단어

→ _____

_____

2 신선한 농산물의 최적의 품질을 달성하는 데 도움이 되도록 기체가 유입될 수도 있다. (Gases, introduce, an optimal quality of, produce) 13단어

→ _____

_____

**A** 우리말은 영어로, 영어는 우리말로 쓰시오.

1 realize _____

2 astonishing _____

3 intriguing _____

4 반사하다 _____

5 혼잡한 _____

6 동시에 _____

**B** 괄호 안의 주어진 단어를 바르게 배열하시오.

1 You are near a focus; a special point (concentrated, the sound, where, from you gets).

→ _____

2 Whispering galleries are acoustic (ceilings, spaces found, curved, beneath).

→ _____

**C** 다음 빈칸에 들어갈 알맞은 단어를 적으시오.

1 지나가는 사람들은 여러분이 하는 말을 듣지 못할 것이다.

The _____ won't hear _____ you are _____.

2 여러분은 분리되어 40피트 떨어져 있으면서도 말을 주고받을 수 있다.

You can exchange words _____ you're _____ and forty feet _____.

**D** 다음 괄호 안의 주어진 단어를 활용하여 문장을 완성하시오.

1 반사되는 음파는 서로를 강화하여 여러분의 말이 들리게 한다. (The reflected, one another, and allow, words, hear) 13단어

→ _____

_____

2 음파는 모든 방향으로 이동하고 벽에서 반사된다. (The sound waves, travel, in, bounce, the walls) 12단어

→ _____

_____

**A** 우리말은 영어로, 영어는 우리말로 쓰시오.

1 last _____

2 length _____

3 adjust _____

4 땀을 흘리다 _____

5 타고난, 고유의 _____

6 통제, 규제 _____

**B** 괄호 안의 주어진 단어를 바르게 배열하시오.

1 We (have, regulation mechanism, intrinsic, an, do).

→ _____

2 There (we, lots of, our temperature, can adjust, are, ways that).

→ _____

**C** 다음 빈칸에 들어갈 알맞은 단어를 적으시오.

1 우리가 어디를 가든, 무엇을 하든, 체온은 유지된다.

_____ we go and _____ we do, the body temperature is _____.

2 중요한 것은 몸의 표면 온도가 아니다.

_____ is not the temperature at the _____ of the body that _____.

**D** 다음 괄호 안의 주어진 단어를 활용하여 문장을 완성하시오.

1 일관되게 유지되어야 하는 것은 몸 속 깊은 곳의 온도이다. (It, the, deep inside, which must, consistent) 13단어

→ _____

2 우리는 우리가 행동하는 방식을 바꿈으로써 체온을 조절할 수 있다. (our temperature, by, the way, behave) 14단어

→ _____

**A** 우리말은 영어로, 영어는 우리말로 쓰시오.

1 time lag _____

2 immediate _____

3 In addition to _____

4 ~처럼 보이다 _____

5 반사, 반영 _____

6 잔상 _____

**B** 괄호 안의 주어진 단어를 바르게 배열하시오.

1 If we had a powerful telescope, (we, around, the dinosaurs, see, would, walking).

→ _____

2 The end of the universe is so (the beginning, that, see, we, be able to, might, old).

→ _____

**C** 다음 빈칸에 들어갈 알맞은 단어를 적으시오.

1 바로 지금은 과학과 거리가 먼 것 같다.

Science _____ _____ _____ a long way from right now.

2 6,000만 광년 떨어진 곳에 위치한 그 별에 우리가 존재한다고 가정해 보라.

_____ that we are on the star _____ sixty million light-years away.

**D** 다음 괄호 안의 주어진 단어를 활용하여 문장을 완성하시오.

1 과학은 세상이 어떻게 우리에게 보이는지를 말해 줄 수 있을 뿐이다. (only tell, appear) 11단어

→ _____

2 우리는 그것들의 이동하는 빛 때문에 여전히 몇몇 별들을 본다. (still see, some of the stars, traveling light) 12단어

→ _____

**A** 우리말은 영어로, 영어는 우리말로 쓰시오.

1 severe _____

2 pick up _____

3 investigation _____

4 받아들이다 _____

5 마지못해 하는, 꺼리는 _____

6 현상 _____

**B** 괄호 안의 주어진 단어를 바르게 배열하시오.

1 She had to count for (felt, she, was, what, one minute).

→ _____

2 The results showed that she felt (actually had, than, had passed, more time).

→ _____

**C** 다음 빈칸에 들어갈 알맞은 단어를 적으시오.

1 그녀는 열이 나면 날수록 더 빨리 숫자를 셌다.

_____ _____ she was, _____ _____ she counted.

2 그녀는 그가 오랫동안 자리를 비웠다고 불평하였다.

She complained _____ him _____ been gone for a long time.

**D** 다음 괄호 안의 주어진 단어를 활용하여 문장을 완성하시오.

1 그 생리학자의 아내는 심각한 독감으로 아프게 되었다. (The, physiologist, become, with) 11단어

→ _____
_____

2 일종의 '생체 시계'가 더 빨라지는 가능성이 있을 지도 모른다. (might, a chance that, some kind of, 'internal clock', run) 13단어

→ _____

**A** 우리말은 영어로, 영어는 우리말로 쓰시오.

1 refuge _____

2 volcanic _____

3 once-plentiful _____

4 도망가다 _____

5 멸종된 _____

6 가라앉다 _____

**B** 괄호 안의 주어진 단어를 바르게 배열하시오.

1 Surviving individuals (were, find, to, shelter, forced, elsewhere).

→ _____

2 Volcanic activity (beneath, sink, caused, the island refuge, to, the waves).

→ _____

**C** 다음 빈칸에 들어갈 알맞은 단어를 적으시오.

1 그 해류는 사람들이 어떤 종류의 안전한 상륙도 하지 못하게 했다.

The currents _____ humans _____ making any kind of safe landing.

2 특별한 섬이 남아 있었는데, 그곳에서 최후의 마지막 집단이 안전을 발견했다.

There _____ a special island, _____ _____ _____ last colony found safety.

**D** 다음 괄호 안의 주어진 단어를 활용하여 문장을 완성하시오.

1 그 새로운 섬 서식지에는 옛 것의 이점들이 없었다. (island home, lack, the benefits, the old) 10단어

→ _____
_____

2 The Great Auk의 것(이야기)보다 더 가혹한 이야기가 없다는 것은 의심의 여지가 없다. (no doubt that, no story, harsh, that of) 16단어

→ _____

**A** 우리말은 영어로, 영어는 우리말로 쓰시오.

1 collect _____

2 curiosity _____

3 specimen _____

4 모양 _____

5 기회 _____

6 깨닫다, 실현하다 _____

**B** 괄호 안의 주어진 단어를 바르게 배열하시오.

1 This will help them (different, to, from, view, the world, see, points of).

→ _____

2 Collecting gives children opportunities to learn skills (be, used, in their, that, can, daily lives).

→ _____

**C** 다음 빈칸에 들어갈 알맞은 단어를 적으시오.

1 그들은 세상에 있는 것들이 서로 관련되어 있음을 깨달을 수도 있다.

They may realize that things in the world are _____ _____ each _____.

2 우표를 수집하는 것은 그들에게 국경일과 같은 역사적 사건들을 보여준다.

Collecting stamps shows them _____ events, _____ _____ national holidays.

**D** 다음 괄호 안의 주어진 단어를 활용하여 문장을 완성하시오.

1 수집을 하는 것은 아이들에게 새로운 세계를 열어줄 수 있다. (open up, worlds, for) 8단어

→ _____

_____

2 아이들은 자신들의 보물들을 크기별로 구성하는 법을 배울 수 있다. (organize, treasures, by) 12단어

→ _____

**A** 우리말은 영어로, 영어는 우리말로 쓰시오.

1 accidental _____

2 inhabitant _____

3 excavation _____

4 상세한 _____

5 위치한 _____

6 약, 대략 _____

**B** 괄호 안의 주어진 단어를 바르게 배열하시오.

1 The city of Pompeii is (a, buried, Roman town-city, partially).

→ _____

2 Pompeii is one of Italy's most popular tourist attractions, (with, people, 2.5 million, visiting, every year)

→ _____

**C** 다음 빈칸에 들어갈 알맞은 단어를 적으시오.

1 Pompeii는 그 화산의 오랜 분출 기간 동안 파괴되고 묻혔다.

Pompeii was _____ and _____ during a long _____ of the volcano.

2 그것은 로마 제국의 전성기 때 삶에 대한 상세한 통찰력을 제공했다.

It has provided a detailed _____ into life _____ _____ _____ _____ the Roman Empire.

**D** 다음 괄호 안의 주어진 단어를 활용하여 문장을 완성하시오.

1 그 분출은 Pompeii를 화산재와 돌 아래로 묻어버렸다. (bury, under, ash) 8단어

→ _____

_____

2 그것의 거주자들에 대한 많은 증거가 발굴 과정에서 소실되었다. (Much of, the evidence of, lose, in) 12단어

→ _____

_____

**A** 우리말은 영어로, 영어는 우리말로 쓰시오.

1  impulse _____

2  intensity _____

3  frequency _____

4  중요한 _____

5  공격적인 _____

6  상관관계 _____

**B** 괄호 안의 주어진 단어를 바르게 배열하시오.

1  He focuses on "combative sports," (which, include, actual, contact, body).

    → _____

2  He discovers a significant relationship (combative, between, sports and violence).

    → _____

**C** 다음 빈칸에 들어갈 알맞은 단어를 적으시오.

1  전투적인 스포츠가 더 많을수록 전투가 일어날 가능성이 더 적다.

    The _____ combative sports, the _____ _____ warfare.

2  어떤 사람은 그것들 사이에 부정적인 상관관계를 찾을 것을 기대한다.

    One would expect _____ _____ a _____ correlation _____ them.

**D** 다음 괄호 안의 주어진 단어를 활용하여 문장을 완성하시오.

1  우리는 스포츠가 폭력을 줄이는 방법이라고 믿는다.
    (a way of, violence) 9단어

    → _____
    _____

2  Sipes는 전투적인 스포츠가 전쟁에 대한 대체물이 아니라는 결론을 도출한다. (the conclusion that, alternatives to) 12단어

    → _____
    _____

**A** 우리말은 영어로, 영어는 우리말로 쓰시오.

1  element _____

2  considerable _____

3  simultaneously _____

4  무형의 _____

5  확고함 _____

6  손이 닿지 않은 _____

**B** 괄호 안의 주어진 단어를 바르게 배열하시오.

1  This confirmation (is, experience, based, on, a physical).

    → _____

2  They experience moments (seen, already, have, that, at home, they) in books.

    → _____

**C** 다음 빈칸에 들어갈 알맞은 단어를 적으시오.

1  문학과 달리, 관광은 '실제', 유형의 세계로 이어진다.

    In _____ _____ literature, tourism _____ _____ 'real', tangible worlds.

2  후자의 경우에도, 그들은 적어도 부분적으로는 상상의 세계 안에 머물러 있다.

    Even in the _____ case, they remain, _____ _____ partly, in an imaginary world.

**D** 다음 괄호 안의 주어진 단어를 활용하여 문장을 완성하시오.

1  신화는 텔레비전보다 훨씬 더 강력한 방식으로 경험된다.
    (The myth, in, much, powerful way, by) 13단어

    → _____
    _____

2  손이 닿지 않은 자연에 대한 그들의 개념은 아마도 확고해질 것이다. (notions of, probably, be) 9단어

    → _____
    _____

**A** 우리말은 영어로, 영어는 우리말로 쓰시오.

1 figure _____

2 fascinated _____

3 unexpected _____

4 도전하다 _____

5 상기시키다 _____

6 내적인, 본질적인 _____

**B** 괄호 안의 주어진 단어를 바르게 배열하시오.

1 His artwork helps (the world, from, you, perspectives, different, see).

→ _____

2 You can get an intrinsic pleasure (have, experienced, you, never, that, before).

→ _____

**C** 다음 빈칸에 들어갈 알맞은 단어를 적으시오.

1 우리는 우리의 전제가 뒤집힐 때 매료된다.

We are _____ when our assumptions are _____ _____ _____.

2 그가 그러한 방식으로 그것을 사용해서 당신은 어떤 것도 이치에 맞지 않다고 생각한다.

He used it in _____ a way _____ you think that nothing _____ _____.

**D** 다음 괄호 안의 주어진 단어를 활용하여 문장을 완성하시오.

1 작품 속의 인물들이 하나로 합쳐진다.
(in the artwork, come) 7단어

→ _____

2 그것은 당신에게 색깔이 대안적인 방식으로 사용될 수 있음을 상기시켜준다. (remind, that, in alternative ways)
11단어

→ _____

---

**A** 우리말은 영어로, 영어는 우리말로 쓰시오.

1 funeral _____

2 interpret _____

3 unfamiliar _____

4 유사성 _____

5 음, 음조 _____

6 본질적으로 _____

**B** 괄호 안의 주어진 단어를 바르게 배열하시오.

1 (is, about, nothing, music, There, inherently sad) music played in a minor key.

→ _____

2 There is a view that finds resemblance in (between, music and emotion, the link).

→ _____

**C** 다음 빈칸에 들어갈 알맞은 단어를 적으시오.

1 우리는 어떤 종류의 음악을 슬프다고 듣게 된다.

We have just _____ _____ _____ certain kinds of music _____ sad.

2 우리는 음악에 표현된 감정을 해석하는 데 어려움을 겪는다.

We _____ difficulty _____ the emotions _____ in music.

**D** 다음 괄호 안의 주어진 단어를 활용하여 문장을 완성하시오.

1 우리가 느린 음악을 들을 때, 우리는 그것을 슬프게 듣는다.
(When, hear, as sad) 10단어

→ _____

2 단순히 학습된 연관성을 통해, 음악은 감정을 표현할 수 있다.
(Simply, a, association, could) 9단어

→ _____

**A** 우리말은 영어로, 영어는 우리말로 쓰시오.

1 indeed _____

2 endless _____

3 comprehensibility _____

4 현대 _____

5 제한적인 _____

6 일반화하다 _____

**B** 괄호 안의 주어진 단어를 바르게 배열하시오.

1 However, painters (at, the colors, use, all, once, don't).

→ _____

2 Mondrian limited (primary, mostly, colors, to, himself, three, the).

→ _____

**C** 다음 빈칸에 들어갈 알맞은 단어를 적으시오.

1 Kasimir Malevich도 비슷한 스스로 부과한 제한으로 작업했다.

Kasimir Malevich worked _____ similar

_____ _____.

2 그리스와 로마인들 빨강, 노랑, 검정, 흰색만을 사용하는 경향이 있었다.

The Greeks and Romans _____ _____ use _____ red, yellow, black and white.

**D** 다음 괄호 안의 주어진 단어를 활용하여 문장을 완성하시오.

1 화가들은 이용 가능한 무한한 범위의 색을 가진다. (Painters, an, range, colors, available) 8단어

→ _____

_____

2 제한된 색들이 명확성과 이해 가능성을 촉진했을 것 같다. (It seems likely that, promote, clarity) 11단어

→ _____

_____

**A** 우리말은 영어로, 영어는 우리말로 쓰시오.

1 material _____

2 reinforce _____

3 circumstance _____

4 작곡가 _____

5 관찰하다 _____

6 실질적인 _____

**B** 괄호 안의 주어진 단어를 바르게 배열하시오.

1 Each new piece (is, to, sure, remain, available).

→ _____

2 It became almost (again, to, it, hear, impossible).

→ _____

**C** 다음 빈칸에 들어갈 알맞은 단어를 적으시오.

1 기존에 작곡된 음악을 다시 이용하는 것이 그것을 더 오래가게 하는 유일한 방법이었다.

_____ previously _____ music was the only way to _____ it more _____.

2 우리는 어떻게 오늘날의 작곡가들이 그렇게 하지 못하게 되는지 관찰할 필요가 있다

We need to _____ how today's composers are _____ _____ _____ so.

**D** 다음 괄호 안의 주어진 단어를 활용하여 문장을 완성하시오.

1 사람들은 많은 음악적 자료를 사실상의 공유물이라고 여겼다. (consider, much, de facto, property) 9단어

→ _____

_____

2 그것은 선율의 순환을 증가시킴으로써 유럽 음악의 전통을 강화할 것이다. (That would, European, by, the circulation, melodies) 12단어

→ _____

_____

| Q | · · · · · · · · · · · · · · · · · · · · · · · · · · · · · · · · · · · · · · · · · · · · · · · · · · · · · · · · · · · · · · · · · · · · · · · · · · · · · · ·

**A** 우리말은 영어로, 영어는 우리말로 쓰시오.

1  namely          _____

2  conflicting     _____

3  shelter         _____

4  안전한          _____

5  침입            _____

6  장래의, 유망한  _____

**B** 괄호 안의 주어진 단어를 바르게 배열하시오.

1  (a modern city, rising every day, The glass buildings, in) are the engineering answer.

→ _____

2  (we, most of, The life, our time, spend) indoors is made light by glass.

→ _____

**C** 다음 빈칸에 들어갈 알맞은 단어를 적으시오.

1  우리는 우리의 건물이 날씨로부터 우리를 보호하기를 기대한다.

We _____ our buildings to _____ us _____ the weather.

2  유리 창문은 우리가 영업 중임을 의미하게 된다.

Glass windows have come to _____ that we are open for _____.

**D** 다음 괄호 안의 주어진 단어를 활용하여 문장을 완성하시오.

1  유리가 없는 현대 도시를 상상하기란 불가능하다.
(It, a modern city, without) 10단어

→ _____

_____

2  가게 유리가 없는 가게는 실질적으로 전혀 가게가 아니다.
(a shop window, practically, not, at all) 13단어

→ _____

_____

---

| 주제별 연습 01 | · · · · · · · · · · · · · · · · · · · · · · · · · · · · · · · · · · · · · · · · · · · · · · · · · · · ·

**A** 우리말은 영어로, 영어는 우리말로 쓰시오.

1  function        _____

2  serve           _____

3  composition     _____

4  왕실의          _____

5  친근한          _____

6  맥락, 상황      _____

**B** 괄호 안의 주어진 단어를 바르게 배열하시오.

1  Our culture (towards, biased, the, arts, fine, is).

→ _____

2  Chamber music really was designed (chambers, be, to, in, performed).

→ _____

**C** 다음 빈칸에 들어갈 알맞은 단어를 적으시오.

1  이러한 구분은 문화적으로 그리고 역사적으로 상대적이다.

This _____ is culturally and historically _____.

2  대부분 현대의 고급 예술(순수 예술)은 일종의 공예로 시작되었다.

Most _____ high art began _____ some kind of _____.

**D** 다음 괄호 안의 주어진 단어를 활용하여 문장을 완성하시오.

1  우리는 이러한 작품들을 순수 예술로 듣는다.
(listen, works, as, fine) 8단어

→ _____

_____

2  Bach에서 Chopin에 이르는 작곡가들에 의해 작곡된 춤곡들은 춤을 동반했다. (The dances that, compose, from, accompany, dancing) 14단어

→ _____

_____

······| 주제별 연습 02 |·································· | 주제별 연습 03 |············

**A** 우리말은 영어로, 영어는 우리말로 쓰시오.

1 eyeline      _____

2 in place of      _____

3 tilt      _____

4 문자 그대로      _____

5 비유적으로      _____

6 기어 다니는      _____

**B** 괄호 안의 주어진 단어를 바르게 배열하시오.

1 The best method may (the floor, lie, to, be, on).

→ _____

2 (it, makes, that, different, All) is the relative height between a young child and an adult.

→ _____

**C** 다음 빈칸에 들어갈 알맞은 단어를 적으시오.

1 그 결과로 생긴 사진은 그 아이를 더 작게 보이게 할 수 있다.

The _____ picture can make the child _____ smaller.

2 카메라가 사진을 찍을 때 더 자연스럽게 보이는 인물 사진들을 얻는 것이 가능하다.

It is _____ to acquire more natural-looking _____ when the camera _____.

**D** 다음 괄호 안의 주어진 단어를 활용하여 문장을 완성하시오.

1 이것은 사진 찍을 때 앉는 것을 의미할 수도 있다. (might, sit down, shooting) 7단어

→ _____

_____

2 아이의 사진을 찍는 것은 어떤 다른 사람의 사진을 찍는 것과 거의 다르지 않다. (Photograph, a child, little, from, person) 11단어

→ _____

_____

**A** 우리말은 영어로, 영어는 우리말로 쓰시오.

1 legal      _____

2 ritual      _____

3 establish      _____

4 확인하다, 식별하다      _____

5 정제하다, 다듬다      _____

6 장소, 환경      _____

**B** 괄호 안의 주어진 단어를 바르게 배열하시오.

1 We do not go backstage in a theater (not specifically, we, if, invited, are).

→ _____

2 Their form and spatial organization give us hints about (be, they, should, how, used).

→ _____

**C** 다음 빈칸에 들어갈 알맞은 단어를 적으시오.

1 이러한 반응들의 강도는 우리의 문화에 의해 결정된다.

The _____ of these _____ ____ _____ by our culture.

2 우리는 인식하고 그 건물들의 기능과 연관시키게 되었다.

We have come to _____ and _____ with those buildings' _____.

**D** 다음 괄호 안의 주어진 단어를 활용하여 문장을 완성하시오.

1 그것들의 물리적 배치는 어떤 사용을 권장하고 다른 것(사용)들을 억제한다. (layout, some uses, restrain, others) 9단어

→ _____

_____

2 건물들은 우리 마음속에 공감할 수 있는 반응을 불러일으킨다. (evoke, empathetic, in our minds) 8단어

→ _____

_____

**A** 우리말은 영어로, 영어는 우리말로 쓰시오.

1 cognitive _____

2 treadmill _____

3 processing _____

4 두 배가 되다 _____

5 시대 _____

6 자금 조달 _____

**B** 괄호 안의 주어진 단어를 바르게 배열하시오.

1 (do here, What, to, trying, we're) is jump start their brains.

→ _____

2 Naperville is looking for (to, kids, new activities, moving, get).

→ _____

**C** 다음 빈칸에 들어갈 알맞은 단어를 적으시오.

1 그 학생들은 실제로 문제 해결을 10%까지 더 잘한다.

The students actually do _____ _____ 10 percent better at _____ _____.

2 복잡한 운동은 사고를 자극한다.

_____ movement _____ thinking.

**D** 다음 괄호 안의 주어진 단어를 활용하여 문장을 완성하시오.

1 체육이 바로 그 날의 첫 수업이다. (Physical education, the very, class, day) 10단어

→ _____

2 수학과 읽기로 고군분투하는 학생들은 먼저 체육 수업을 받으러 간다. (The, who, struggle with, reading, gym class, first) 13단어

→ _____

**A** 우리말은 영어로, 영어는 우리말로 쓰시오.

1 especially _____

2 application _____

3 résumé _____

4 근본적인 _____

5 나누다 _____

6 넓히다 _____

**B** 괄호 안의 주어진 단어를 바르게 배열하시오.

1 People can form (personal, of, a wide, relationships, range).

→ _____

2 They take part in school activities (of, a, reasons, for, number, very good).

→ _____

**C** 다음 빈칸에 들어갈 알맞은 단어를 적으시오.

1 때때로 학생들은 과외 활동에 참여한다.

From time to time, students _____ _____ _____ activities.

2 당신의 가까운 사회적 집단 속에 있지 않은 사람들과 사귀는 것은 재미있을 수 있다.

It can be exciting to _____ _____ _____ people who are not in your _____ social _____.

**D** 다음 괄호 안의 주어진 단어를 활용하여 문장을 완성하시오.

1 그들은 자신들이 추구하고 싶은 관심사를 가지고 있다. (interests, that, wish, pursue) 8단어

→ _____

2 당신과 다를지도 모르는 새로운 사람들과 만나는 것은 재미있다. (Meeting, who, might, different, fun) 11단어

→ _____

**A 우리말은 영어로, 영어는 우리말로 쓰시오.**

1 senior school _____

2 besides _____

3 local _____

4 몇몇의, 몇 가지 _____

5 초등학교 _____

6 언어학자 _____

**B 괄호 안의 주어진 단어를 바르게 배열하시오.**

1 They listened out for (in, the slang, used, their school).
→ _____

2 (it, would ever, about, There's, way, I, know about, no) if you did not tell me what it was.
→ _____

**C 다음 빈칸에 들어갈 알맞은 단어를 적으시오.**

1 단 한 학교 내에서 다르게 사용되는 어휘가 심지어 있을 수도 있다.
There may even be words _____ differently _____ a _____ school.

2 각각의 학교에서 들리는 은어의 종류에 종종 차이점이 있다.
There are often _____ in the kind of slang which ____ _____ in _____ school.

**D 다음 괄호 안의 주어진 단어를 활용하여 문장을 완성하시오.**

1 은어는 언어학자들이 파악하기가 사실 꽤 어렵다. (Slang, actually, quite, for, find out about) 11단어
→ _____

2 1학년 학생들에 의해서 사용되는 은어는 그들 자신의 것과 매우 달랐다. (The slang, which, use, first-year, own) 14단어
→ _____

**A 우리말은 영어로, 영어는 우리말로 쓰시오.**

1 summit _____

2 innovate _____

3 territory _____

4 조직의, 단체의 _____

5 요구하다 _____

6 내적인, 내부의 _____

**B 괄호 안의 주어진 단어를 바르게 배열하시오.**

1 You'll tell me it was a time (at, that, felt, you, risk).
→ _____

2 Those are the places (to, in which, are, opportunities, improve, there).
→ _____

**C 다음 빈칸에 들어갈 알맞은 단어를 적으시오.**

1 당신은 일을 하는 전통적인 방법에 이의를 제기해야 한다.
You have to _____ the _____ ways of doing things.

2 당신은 현재 경험의 경계선을 넘어서 위험을 무릅써야 한다.
You have to _____ beyond the _____ of your _____ experience.

**D 다음 괄호 안의 주어진 단어를 활용하여 문장을 완성하시오.**

1 성장은 항상 가장자리에 있다. (Growth, at, edges) 6단어
→ _____

2 당신은 자신의 안전지대를 벗어나서 독립해야 한다. (have to, get out of, comfort zone, and, become) 12단어
→ _____

**A 우리말은 영어로, 영어는 우리말로 쓰시오.**

1 statement _____

2 regardless of _____

3 literary _____

4 함축 _____

5 해석하다 _____

6 배제하다 _____

**B 괄호 안의 주어진 단어를 바르게 배열하시오.**

1 (What, gives us, implies, a text) great interest.

→ _____

2 We should ask what the text (literary, suggests, to approach, as a way, interpretation).

→ _____

**C 다음 빈칸에 들어갈 알맞은 단어를 적으시오.**

1 그것들은 자신들의 주장에 대해 직접적으로 말하기보다는 함축한다.

They imply _____ _____ talk about their _____ directly.

2 문학 작품은 암시(의 양)보다 더 많은 양의 직접적인 말하기를 포함할 수도 있다.

Literary works may _____ larger _____ of direct telling _____ _____ of suggestion.

**D 다음 괄호 안의 주어진 단어를 활용하여 문장을 완성하시오.**

1 우리는 글을 이해하는 기량을 얻게 된다. (gain, practice, in, make sense, texts) 8단어

→ _____
_____

2 글의 함축들을 알아내는 우리의 작업은 우리의 분석적 능력을 시험한다. (work of, figure out, a text's, test, analytical powers) 12단어

→ _____

**A 우리말은 영어로, 영어는 우리말로 쓰시오.**

1 bond _____

2 terms _____

3 agreement _____

4 편리한 _____

5 진화의 _____

6 구체적인 _____

**B 괄호 안의 주어진 단어를 바르게 배열하시오.**

1 This is (plays, where, a key role, conversation).

→ _____

2 Language is convenient (you, trying, are, when, conduct, to, business) with someone.

→ _____

**C 다음 빈칸에 들어갈 알맞은 단어를 적으시오.**

1 우리는 거래하기 위해서 신뢰를 확립할 필요가 있었다.

We needed to _____ trust _____ _____ _____ trade.

2 언어는 구체적인 것을 표현함으로써 우리가 합의에 이르게 한다.

Language _____ us to reach a consensus _____ _____ the specific.

**D 다음 괄호 안의 주어진 단어를 활용하여 문장을 완성하시오.**

1 몸짓만을 사용해서는 그 상업 거래가 거의 불가능했을 것이다. (That, would have, nearly, using, gestures) 11단어

→ _____

2 많은 생물학자들은 인간이 경제적인 이유로 언어를 발달시켰다고 주장한다. (Many, argue that, develop, reasons) 10단어

→ _____

**A** 우리말은 영어로, 영어는 우리말로 쓰시오.

1  imply　　　　＿＿＿＿＿＿＿＿＿＿＿＿＿＿

2  quantity　　　＿＿＿＿＿＿＿＿＿＿＿＿＿＿

3  intention　　 ＿＿＿＿＿＿＿＿＿＿＿＿＿＿

4  관점, 시각　　 ＿＿＿＿＿＿＿＿＿＿＿＿＿＿

5  많이 읽는, 다독의　＿＿＿＿＿＿＿＿＿＿＿＿

6  비판적인　　　＿＿＿＿＿＿＿＿＿＿＿＿＿＿

**B** 괄호 안의 주어진 단어를 바르게 배열하시오.

1  It's not an inborn (but, you, develop, skill that, a learned, will).
→ ＿＿＿＿＿＿＿＿＿＿＿＿＿＿＿＿＿＿＿

2  There's a difference between (and knowing, to read well, how, being well-read).
→ ＿＿＿＿＿＿＿＿＿＿＿＿＿＿＿＿＿＿＿

**C** 다음 빈칸에 들어갈 알맞은 단어를 적으시오.

1  그것은 중요한 것은 양이 아니라 질이라는 것을 의미한다.
It means that it's ＿＿＿ ＿＿＿＿＿＿ ＿＿＿ quality that ＿＿＿＿＿.

2  당신은 어떤 사람들이 다독을 한다고 언급되는 것을 들었을지도 모른다.
You may have heard certain people ＿＿＿＿＿＿ ＿＿＿ ＿＿＿ being well-read.

**D** 다음 괄호 안의 주어진 단어를 활용하여 문장을 완성하시오.

1  비판적 읽기는 당신이 문학을 대단히 깊이 있게 볼 수 있도록 할 것이다. (enable, look at, great depth) 12단어
→ ＿＿＿＿＿＿＿＿＿＿＿＿＿＿＿＿＿＿＿
＿＿＿＿＿＿＿＿＿＿＿＿＿＿＿＿＿＿＿＿

2  그것은 당신 앞에 있는 글로 쓰인 자료에 관해 당신이 생각할 것을 요구한다. (It, require, that, the, material, in front of) 13단어
→ ＿＿＿＿＿＿＿＿＿＿＿＿＿＿＿＿＿＿＿
＿＿＿＿＿＿＿＿＿＿＿＿＿＿＿＿＿＿＿＿

**A** 우리말은 영어로, 영어는 우리말로 쓰시오.

1  analogy　　　＿＿＿＿＿＿＿＿＿＿＿＿＿＿

2  suppose　　　＿＿＿＿＿＿＿＿＿＿＿＿＿＿

3  constituent　 ＿＿＿＿＿＿＿＿＿＿＿＿＿＿

4  나타내다　　　＿＿＿＿＿＿＿＿＿＿＿＿＿＿

5  구조적인　　　＿＿＿＿＿＿＿＿＿＿＿＿＿＿

6  유사성　　　　＿＿＿＿＿＿＿＿＿＿＿＿＿＿

**B** 괄호 안의 주어진 단어를 바르게 배열하시오.

1  It doesn't mean (such, that, a structure, has, the thought itself).
→ ＿＿＿＿＿＿＿＿＿＿＿＿＿＿＿＿＿＿＿

2  (similarities, what is representing, There, between, are) and what is represented.
→ ＿＿＿＿＿＿＿＿＿＿＿＿＿＿＿＿＿＿＿

**C** 다음 빈칸에 들어갈 알맞은 단어를 적으시오.

1  어떤 생각은 특정한 언어적 구조를 가진 말로 표현될 수도 있다.
A thought might ＿＿＿＿＿ ＿＿＿＿＿＿ verbally ＿＿＿＿＿ a particular linguistic ＿＿＿＿＿.

2  그 단어에 상응하는 물체도 세계나 나의 시각적 이미지에 존재하지 않는다.
There exists no object ＿＿＿＿＿＿＿＿ ＿＿＿＿ the word ＿＿＿＿＿ in the world ＿＿＿＿ in my visual image.

**D** 다음 괄호 안의 주어진 단어를 활용하여 문장을 완성하시오.

1  그는 '숫자들'의 표현으로 한 가지 비유를 제시한다.
(with the representation of) 9단어
→ ＿＿＿＿＿＿＿＿＿＿＿＿＿＿＿＿＿＿＿
＿＿＿＿＿＿＿＿＿＿＿＿＿＿＿＿＿＿＿＿

2  내가 보는 것은 몇 개의 과일과 그릇 하나를 포함한다.
(What, see, some, a bowl) 11단어
→ ＿＿＿＿＿＿＿＿＿＿＿＿＿＿＿＿＿＿＿
＿＿＿＿＿＿＿＿＿＿＿＿＿＿＿＿＿＿＿＿

# >UNIT 11 정보, 미디어

## A 우리말은 영어로, 영어는 우리말로 쓰시오.

1 wound _____

2 consistently _____

3 intended _____

4 ~에 의지하다 _____

5 대중; 공공의 _____

6 물러나다; 후퇴 _____

## B 괄호 안의 주어진 단어를 바르게 배열하시오.

1 (German, attacks on, rocket-bomb, The, London) suddenly escalated.

→ _____

2 They relied (secret, had planted, agents they, on) in England.

→ _____

## C 다음 빈칸에 들어갈 알맞은 단어를 적으시오.

1 그들은 이 비밀요원들이 영국에 의해 발각되었던 것을 알지 못했다.

They did not know that these agents _____ _____ _____ by England.

2 그 폭탄들은 그것들이 떨어질 때마다 목표물에서 점점 더 먼 곳에 맞히곤 했다.

The bombs _____ hit farther and farther from their targets _____ they fell.

## D 다음 괄호 안의 주어진 단어를 활용하여 문장을 완성하시오.

1 2,000개가 넘는 비행 폭탄들은 5,000명 이상의 사람들을 죽였다. (over, flying bombs, more than) 11단어

→ _____

_____

2 영국에 의해 조종되는 요원들은 그들에게 교묘히 거짓된 정보를 주고 있었다. (English-controlled, subtly, deceptive) 8단어

→ _____

_____

## A 우리말은 영어로, 영어는 우리말로 쓰시오.

1 handwritten _____

2 scarce _____

3 contribution _____

4 결과적으로 _____

5 호의적인 _____

6 동등한 _____

## B 괄호 안의 주어진 단어를 바르게 배열하시오.

1 Very few individuals (study, to, had, Latin, the opportunity).

→ _____

2 They rapidly (Latin, as, replaced, the medium) of discourse.

→ _____

## C 다음 빈칸에 들어갈 알맞은 단어를 적으시오.

1 유럽의 과학과 일반적인 지식은 라틴어로 기록되었다.

European science and general _____ were _____ in Latin.

2 유럽에서의 과학적 창의력의 거대한 폭발은 정보를 확산시키는 것을 도왔다.

The great _____ of scientific creativity in Europe helped _____ information.

## D 다음 괄호 안의 주어진 단어를 활용하여 문장을 완성하시오.

1 라틴어는 그때 당시에 더 이상 아무도 말하지 않는 언어였다. (no one, speak, longer, that time) 13단어

→ _____

_____

2 구텐베르크는 인쇄술에서 가동 활자를 발명하였는데, 그것은 일상 언어들의 수용을 이끌었다. (Gutenberg, which, the acceptance, everyday languages) 14단어

→ _____

_____

**A 우리말은 영어로, 영어는 우리말로 쓰시오.**

1 upcoming _____

2 account _____

3 chance _____

4 줄이다 _____

5 양 _____

6 홍보하다, 촉진시키다 _____

**B 괄호 안의 주어진 단어를 바르게 배열하시오.**

1 A great comedian (day, hours each, her skill, working, spends, on).

→ _____

2 The comedian (people, the chances, could, increase, that) will buy tickets.

→ _____

**C 다음 빈칸에 들어갈 알맞은 단어를 적으시오.**

1 어느 유명한 코미디언은 그녀의 Instagram 팔로잉에 대해 질문을 계속 받는다.

A great comedian keeps _____ _____ about her Instagram following.

2 당신은 그것에 적응할 필요가 있는데 그렇지 않은 사람들은 성공하지 못할 것이기 때문이다.

You need to _____ to it because _____ who don't won't succeed.

**D 다음 괄호 안의 주어진 단어를 활용하여 문장을 완성하시오.**

1 이것은 그 쇼를 홍보하는데 쓰이는 돈의 양을 줄인다. (reduce, the amount, promote) 11단어

→ _____

_____

2 사람들은 팔로워 수가 재능보다 더 중요한 것처럼 보이는 것을 걱정한다. (worried, that, count, seem) 13단어

→ _____

**A 우리말은 영어로, 영어는 우리말로 쓰시오.**

1 threaten _____

2 justify _____

3 question _____

4 수행하다, 공연하다 _____

5 중대한, 중요한 _____

6 진보적인 _____

**B 괄호 안의 주어진 단어를 바르게 배열하시오.**

1 War should be (the last, all, other options, resort when) have failed.

→ _____

2 Unfortunately, (to perform, fail, often, the media) this crucial role.

→ _____

**C 다음 빈칸에 들어갈 알맞은 단어를 적으시오.**

1 대중들은 상황들의 다른 측면을 볼 수 있다.

The _____ can see the other _____ of things.

2 그들은 언제나 대중의 이익을 위한 파수꾼이진 않았다.

They have _____ _____ been watchdogs for the public _____.

**D 다음 괄호 안의 주어진 단어를 활용하여 문장을 완성하시오.**

1 그것들은 가장 철저한 조사를 제공하고 있어야 한다. (should, provide, intense scrutiny) 8단어

→ _____

_____

2 그들 자신의 몇몇 주요 사안들에 대한 보도는 때때로 눈에 띄게 편향적인 것처럼 보인다. (coverage, major, one-sided, at times) 12단어

→ _____

# 12 컴퓨터, 인터넷, 교통

**A** 우리말은 영어로, 영어는 우리말로 쓰시오.

1 aspect _____

2 lack _____

3 output _____

4 초과하다, 넘다 _____

5 합, 총합 _____

6 지능, 지성 _____

**B** 괄호 안의 주어진 단어를 바르게 배열하시오.

1 Conversely, (cannot, a computer, decisions, independent, make).

→ _____

2 The initial programming (done, must, be, by humans).

→ _____

**C** 다음 빈칸에 들어갈 알맞은 단어를 적으시오.

1 프로그램되지 않으면 문제 해결을 위한 단계들을 만들어 내지 못한다.

It fails to _____ steps for solving problems ____ _____ programmed.

2 이러한 기계들의 강점과 인간의 그것들(강점)을 결합하는 것은 시너지를 창조한다.

_____ the strengths of these machines _____ _____ of humans' creates synergy.

**D** 다음 괄호 안의 주어진 단어를 활용하여 문장을 완성하시오.

1 컴퓨터는 사람들보다 훨씬 더 대단한 속도로 정확히 데이터를 처리할 수 있다. (process, far, speeds) 11단어

→ _____

2 인간들은 상대적으로 느리게 일하고 실수를 하는 반면에 컴퓨터는 빠르고 정확하게 작동한다. (A computer, quickly, while, slowly, mistakes) 14단어

→ _____

**A** 우리말은 영어로, 영어는 우리말로 쓰시오.

1 violate _____

2 privacy _____

3 accumulate _____

4 저장하다; 상점 _____

5 이익을 주다 _____

6 개인, 사람 _____

**B** 괄호 안의 주어진 단어를 바르게 배열하시오.

1 Favorite websites (users, like, old friends, sometimes, welcome).

→ _____

2 On the bright side, (greatly benefit, can, cookies, individuals).

→ _____

**C** 다음 빈칸에 들어갈 알맞은 단어를 적으시오.

1 온라인 서점들은 이름을 대면서 고객들에게 인사하고 새로운 책들을 제안한다.

Online bookstores _____ their customers by name and _____ new books.

2 쿠키는 해커들에게 시스템에 침입할 많은 방법들을 제공한다.

Cookies _____ hackers many ways to _____ into systems.

**D** 다음 괄호 안의 주어진 단어를 활용하여 문장을 완성하시오.

1 부동산 사이트들은 새로운 부동산들로 그들의 방문자들을 안내한다. (guide, properties) 9단어

→ _____

2 그것들은 인터넷 서버가 개인들의 웹브라우저 내부에 저장하는 작은 파일들이다. (that, stores, inside, browsers) 13단어

→ _____

**A 우리말은 영어로, 영어는 우리말로 쓰시오.**

1 separate _____

2 opposite _____

3 direction _____

4 평가하다 _____

5 상태, 지위 _____

6 오작동 _____

**B 괄호 안의 주어진 단어를 바르게 배열하시오.**

1 Commercial airplanes (similar, airways which, are, in, travel) to roads.

→ _____

2 Collisions between airplanes (surrounding, occur, the area, usually, in, airports).

→ _____

**C 다음 빈칸에 들어갈 알맞은 단어를 적으시오.**

1 항공기의 수직적 분리는 일부 비행기들이 공항 위로 통과하는 것을 가능하게 한다.

Vertical _____ of aircraft enables some flights to _____ over airports.

2 조종사들은 근처의 비행기들을 탐색하는 것보다 항공기의 상태를 평가하는데 더 많은 시간을 보낸다.

Pilots spend more time _____ aircraft status than searching out _____ planes.

**D 다음 괄호 안의 주어진 단어를 활용하여 문장을 완성하시오.**

1 항공(비행)은 보통 장거리를 다니며, 두 가지 유형의 이동(방식)이 있다. (Air flights, and, travel) 13단어

→ _____

_____

2 항공기 오작동으로 인한 추락들은 장거리 비행들 중에 발생하는 경향이 있다. (due to, aircraft, during, long-haul) 11단어

→ _____

_____

**A 우리말은 영어로, 영어는 우리말로 쓰시오.**

1 obtain _____

2 rapid _____

3 hence _____

4 글, 기사 _____

5 추상적인 _____

6 절대적인, 확실한 _____

**B 괄호 안의 주어진 단어를 바르게 배열하시오.**

1 The Internet (us, rapid, could offer, acquisition, the) of new information.

→ _____

2 What we often get (summaries, abstract, are, no more, than) of long articles.

→ _____

**C 다음 빈칸에 들어갈 알맞은 단어를 적으시오.**

1 사람들은 처음부터 끝까지 전체 논문을 읽어 오고 있었다.

People have been reading the _____ article from beginning to _____.

2 나는 절대적인 고독 속에서 24시간을 지내볼 것을 추천한다.

I recommend _____ you try spending twenty-four hours in absolute _____.

**D 다음 괄호 안의 주어진 단어를 활용하여 문장을 완성하시오.**

1 정보의 정확성에 대한 조사는 간단한 문제가 아니다. (The examination, the accuracy, matter) 12단어

→ _____

_____

2 나는 인터넷, 전화, 그리고 다른 장치들의 연결을 끊어볼 것을 추천한다. (that, disconnect, and, devices) 11단어

→ _____

_____

| Q | ·························· | 주제별 연습 01 | ··················

**A** 우리말은 영어로, 영어는 우리말로 쓰시오.

1 celebrity _____

2 consider _____

3 occasional _____

4 다가가다; 접근 _____

5 평균의; 평균 _____

6 호감적인 _____

**B** 괄호 안의 주어진 단어를 바르게 배열하시오.

1 Celebrities are (competent, individuals, generally considered, to be).

→ _____

2 Perfection creates (that, a, the general public, distance, perceived) cannot relate to.

→ _____

**C** 다음 빈칸에 들어갈 알맞은 단어를 적으시오.

1 개인들의 인지된 매력도는 그들이 실수를 한 후에 증가하거나 감소한다.

Individuals' _____ attractiveness _____ or decreases after they make a mistake.

2 실수를 전혀 저지르지 않는 사람들은 덜 매력적이라고 인지된다.

Those _____ never make mistakes are perceived as _____ _____ attractive.

**D** 다음 괄호 안의 주어진 단어를 활용하여 문장을 완성하시오.

1 그것은 그들의 인간미가 다른 사람들에게 사랑 받도록 할 것이다. (make, endearing, others) 8단어

→ _____

_____

2 실수를 전혀 저지르지 않는 사람들은 다가가기 어렵다고 인지된다. (those, never, perceive, be) 12단어

→ _____

_____

**A** 우리말은 영어로, 영어는 우리말로 쓰시오.

1 assumption _____

2 base _____

3 dominant _____

4 공격적인 _____

5 폭력(성) _____

6 탐욕 _____

**B** 괄호 안의 주어진 단어를 바르게 배열하시오.

1 They inadvertently (studies that supported, research, designed) their own thinking.

→ _____

2 It is always (to eruptions, of, violence, vulnerable, greed,) and selfishness.

→ _____

**C** 다음 빈칸에 들어갈 알맞은 단어를 적으시오.

1 인간들은 이기적인 사욕과 같은 저급한 동기들에 의해 움직여진다.

Humans are _____ by base motivations _____ _____ egoistic self-interest.

2 사회적 상호 작용은 그러한 더 저급한 감정들에 통제를 가함으로써 가능하다.

Social _____ is possible by exerting control _____ those baser emotions.

**D** 다음 괄호 안의 주어진 단어를 활용하여 문장을 완성하시오.

1 사람들은 그들의 공격적 성향을 가까스로 억제한다. (barely, keep, tendencies) 8단어

→ _____

_____

2 그 사실은 미약한 합의라고 여겨져 왔다. (have, see, arrangement) 9단어

→ _____

_____

| 주제별 연습 02 |

**A** 우리말은 영어로, 영어는 우리말로 쓰시오.

1 meaningful _____

2 conversation _____

3 prevention _____

4 자살; 자살하다 _____

5 교류, 교환 _____

6 관심, 돌봄 _____

**B** 괄호 안의 주어진 단어를 바르게 배열하시오.

1 He considered (conversation, meaningful, as, a valuable way).

→ _____

2 I am no longer (because, about, thinking, suicide) people care about me.

→ _____

**C** 다음 빈칸에 들어갈 알맞은 단어를 적으시오.

1 외롭지 않기 위한 몇몇 방법들을 찾는 것은 더 좋다.

It's _____ to find some ways to not be _____.

2 난 누군가가 진정으로 관계를 원할 때 들어주는 사람으로서 대단한 기쁨을 느낀다.

I feel a great joy _____ the listener when someone really hopes for _____.

**D** 다음 괄호 안의 주어진 단어를 활용하여 문장을 완성하시오.

1 외로움은 나이와 함께 당신의 삶에 스며들 수 있다. (creep, age) 8단어

→ _____

2 자원봉사자들은 잠재적으로 자살하려는 노인들에게 연락을 한다. (reach out, suicidal seniors) 7단어

→ _____

| 주제별 연습 03 |

**A** 우리말은 영어로, 영어는 우리말로 쓰시오.

1 motivated _____

2 maintain _____

3 influence _____

4 받아들이다 _____

5 환경, 상황 _____

6 독립적인 _____

**B** 괄호 안의 주어진 단어를 바르게 배열하시오.

1 The use of control (ultimately concentrated, is, on, the individual).

→ _____

2 East Asians (to, social support, prefer, more, receive).

→ _____

**C** 다음 빈칸에 들어갈 알맞은 단어를 적으시오.

1 개인의 성공들은 주로 그들 자신의 능력들과 행동들에 달려 있다.

_____ successes depend primarily on their _____ abilities and actions.

2 사람들은 관계 속에서 화합을 증진하는 방식으로 대처하는 것을 선호할 것이다.

People might like to _____ in a way that promotes _____ in relationships.

**D** 다음 괄호 안의 주어진 단어를 활용하여 문장을 완성하시오.

1 이런 것들은 그들의 자아 존중감의 토대 역할을 한다. (serve, the basis, self-worth) 8단어

→ _____

2 사람들은 집단 목표와 화합 쪽에 더 동기부여를 받는 경향이 있다. (tend, motivate, towards, goals) 11단어

→ _____

| Q | ···················· | 주제별 연습 01 | ····················

**A 우리말은 영어로, 영어는 우리말로 쓰시오.**

1 attitude        _____

2 equality      _____

3 mutual       _____

4 편견          _____

5 꺼려하다, 주저하다  _____

6 반대하다      _____

**B 괄호 안의 주어진 단어를 바르게 배열하시오.**

1 It is (norms, backed, social, by) that promote equality.

→ _____

2 They feel that (so, simply inappropriate, is, doing).

→ _____

**C 다음 빈칸에 들어갈 알맞은 단어를 적으시오.**

1 집단 간의 접촉은 지지받지 않는 접촉보다 긍정적인 변화들을 만들 가능성이 더 크다.

Intergroup contact is more _____ to produce _____ changes than unsupported contact.

2 학생들은 어떤 교사들에 의해 행해진 수업에서 더 많이 동기를 부여받았다.

Students were more highly _____ in classes _____ by some teachers.

**D 다음 괄호 안의 주어진 단어를 활용하여 문장을 완성하시오.**

1 그 접촉은 태도를 바꿀 더 큰 가능성을 갖는다.
(contact, great, attitudes) 9단어

→ _____

_____

2 집단들 간의 접촉은 적절하게 보여질 가능성이 더 크다.
(between, likely, see, appropriate) 11단어

→ _____

**A 우리말은 영어로, 영어는 우리말로 쓰시오.**

1 theory        _____

2 consumption   _____

3 status         _____

4 증거          _____

5 일시적인, 임시의    _____

6 남아 있는      _____

**B 괄호 안의 주어진 단어를 바르게 배열하시오.**

1 Demand for them (their, price rises, increases, as).

→ _____

2 The seller (a, temporary, increase, might experience) in sales.

→ _____

**C 다음 빈칸에 들어갈 알맞은 단어를 적으시오.**

1 Veblen에 따르면, 이러한 물건들은 높은 지위를 나타내야 한다.

_____ _____ Veblen, these goods must signal high _____.

2 진정한 베블런재는 더 낮은 가격의 것(물건)보다 눈에 띄게 더 높은 품질은 않을 것이다.

A true Veblen good might not be noticeably higher _____ than lower-priced _____.

**D 다음 괄호 안의 주어진 단어를 활용하여 문장을 완성하시오.**

1 더 높은 가격을 지불하고자 하는 의사는 욕망에 기인한다.
(A willingness, high, due to, a desire) 11단어

→ _____

_____

2 시장 속에서 이런 행동에 대한 많은 증거가 있다.
(there, much, the markets) 10단어

→ _____

_____

**A 우리말은 영어로, 영어는 우리말로 쓰시오.**

1 generate     _____

2 overcome     _____

3 diversify     _____

4 제한하다     _____

5 배제하다, 제외하다     _____

6 자본, 수도     _____

**B 괄호 안의 주어진 단어를 바르게 배열하시오.**

1 It generates (lower, variety, a, of production) and a lower rate of growth.

→ _____

2 They suffer from (restrict, of problems, a series, which) their development.

→ _____

**C 다음 빈칸에 들어갈 알맞은 단어를 적으시오.**

1 일부 개발도상국들은 그들의 천연자원에 지나치게 의존하는 경향이 있다.

Some developing countries tend to depend _____ on their _____ resources.

2 자연자본(천연자원)에 대한 심한 의존은 다른 유형들의 자본을 배제하는 경향이 있다.

A heavy reliance on natural _____ tends to exclude other _____ of capital.

**D 다음 괄호 안의 주어진 단어를 활용하여 문장을 완성하시오.**

1 자원의 풍요는 어떤 해를 입힐 필요가 없다. (resource, need, harm) 7단어

→ _____

_____

2 개발도상국들은 많은 천연자원에 대한 그들의 의존에 갇혀 있다. (trap, dependence, large, resources) 11단어

→ _____

_____

**A 우리말은 영어로, 영어는 우리말로 쓰시오.**

1 distract     _____

2 confuse     _____

3 concern     _____

4 현재(의); 제시하다     _____

5 결정하다, 결심하다     _____

6 작곡가     _____

**B 괄호 안의 주어진 단어를 바르게 배열하시오.**

1 The leaders might have great (coping, with, too many, difficulty, inputs).

→ _____

2 The merits of leaders' important decisions (not, typically are, clear, very).

→ _____

**C 다음 빈칸에 들어갈 알맞은 단어를 적으시오.**

1 현재의 우려는 더 멀리 떨어져 있는 것들(우려들)보다 더 커 보인다.

Concerns of _____ _____ seem larger than _____ farther away.

2 그러한 결정들은 상충되는 이익들에 중요성을 부여하는 것을 포함해야 한다.

Those decisions have to _____ assigning weights to _____ interests.

**D 다음 괄호 안의 주어진 단어를 활용하여 문장을 완성하시오.**

1 지도자들에 의한 몇몇 결정들은 대단한 복잡성을 제시한다. (present, complexity) 7단어

→ _____

_____

2 그것은 베토벤이 브람스보다 더 훌륭한 작곡가라고 말하는 것과 같다. (like, say, that, Beethoven, Brahms) 12단어

→ _____

_____

**A** 우리말은 영어로, 영어는 우리말로 쓰시오.

1 distribution _____

2 relate to _____

3 norm _____

4 유동성 _____

5 꺼리는 _____

6 저항, 반대 _____

**B** 괄호 안의 주어진 단어를 바르게 배열하시오.

1 A hierarchical division (is, convenience only, one of, seen, as).

→ _____

2 (individuals, move up, relatively easy, to, is, for, It) the social hierarchy.

→ _____

**C** 다음 빈칸에 들어갈 알맞은 단어를 적으시오.

1 사람들은 불평등이 아주 적어야 한다고 믿는다.

People believe that _____ should be _____.

2 모든 사람이 사회 계층 내에서 명확히 규정되거나 할당된 위치를 가진다.

Everyone has a clearly _____ or _____ place in the social hierarchy.

**D** 다음 괄호 안의 주어진 단어를 활용하여 문장을 완성하시오.

1 권력 거리에 대한 낮은 수용이 있다.
(acceptance, of, power distance) 7단어

→ _____
_____

2 사회의 권력이 더 적은 구성원들은 자신들의 권력에서의 불평등을 수용한다. (less, powerful, members, inequality, in) 12단어

→ _____
_____

**A** 우리말은 영어로, 영어는 우리말로 쓰시오.

1 economic _____

2 concept _____

3 theory _____

4 빈곤 _____

5 생산성 _____

6 존재하다 _____

**B** 괄호 안의 주어진 단어를 바르게 배열하시오.

1 Employers will be able to exploit workers (not legally, they, controlled, are, if).

→ _____

2 Employers are taking advantage of the law (more, reap, so, can, they, benefits, that).

→ _____

**C** 다음 빈칸에 들어갈 알맞은 단어를 적으시오.

1 최저임금법이 현존하는 시장 실패를 수정하는 원천이다.

_____ wage laws are a _____ of correcting for existing _____ _____.

2 역사적인 증거는 적절한 법의 부재 시 착취당하는 노동자들을 가리킨다.

Historical _____ points to workers _____ in the _____ of _____ laws.

**D** 다음 괄호 안의 주어진 단어를 활용하여 문장을 완성하시오.

1 노동자들이 그들의 공헌에 대해 항상 보상받는 것은 아니다.
(Worker, always, compensate, contributions) 8단어

→ _____

2 그것들은 효율적인 결과를 창출해내는 시장의 힘을 강화시키고 있다. (enhance, the power, markets, create, results) 11단어

→ _____

······ | 주제별 연습 02 | ·······   ······ | 주제별 연습 03 | ·······

**A 우리말은 영어로, 영어는 우리말로 쓰시오.**

1 disrupt _____

2 sue _____

3 aircraft _____

4 제조사 _____

5 개입하다 _____

6 나아가다, 항해하다 _____

**B 괄호 안의 주어진 단어를 바르게 배열하시오.**

1 They want to create new technologies (existing, based, ones, on).

→ _____

2 The original idea of a patent was not to (monopoly, with, inventors, reward, profits).

→ _____

**C 다음 빈칸에 들어갈 알맞은 단어를 적으시오.**

1 어느 정도의 지적재산권법은 분명히 필요하다.

A certain amount of _____ _____ law is plainly _____.

2 대부분의 특허권은 아이디어를 공유하는 것만큼 독점을 옹호하는 것에 관한 것이다.

Most _____ are as _____ about defending _____ as about sharing ideas.

**D 다음 괄호 안의 주어진 단어를 활용하여 문장을 완성하시오.**

1 많은 회사들은 특허권을 진입 장벽으로 사용한다. (firms, patents, as, barriers, entry) 8단어

→ _____

_____

2 오늘날 스마트폰과 생명공학에서도 거의 동일한 상황이 발생했다. (Much, the same, have, happen, with, biotechnology) 10단어

→ _____

_____

**A 우리말은 영어로, 영어는 우리말로 쓰시오.**

1 current _____

2 respect _____

3 eliminate _____

4 결정하다, 결심하다 _____

5 유지하다 _____

6 타협 _____

**B 괄호 안의 주어진 단어를 바르게 배열하시오.**

1 A new social situation is created (in, new, that, emerge, challenges).

→ _____

2 They support one another in the pursuit of (not always, allocated, which, be, goals, may).

→ _____

**C 다음 빈칸에 들어갈 알맞은 단어를 적으시오.**

1 오늘날 미국에서 인종 및 민족의 관계는 과거보다 더 나아졌다.

_____ and _____ relations in the United States are _____ today than in the past.

2 그들은 다양한 문화적 관점들에도 불구하고 서로 함께 일한다.

They work with each other _____ _____ ____ a _____ of cultural _____.

**D 다음 괄호 안의 주어진 단어를 활용하여 문장을 완성하시오.**

1 이러한 난제에 대응하는 것은 평등한 대우에 관한 헌신을 필요로 한다. (Meeting, require, commitment to, treatment) 9단어

→ _____

_____

2 스포츠가 통합과 공정성의 모델이 될 수 있기에 앞서 많은 변화들이 요구된다. (Many, need, before, a model, inclusion) 14단어

→ _____

_____

| Q | ·············································· | 주제별 연습 01 | ··············································

**A** 우리말은 영어로, 영어는 우리말로 쓰시오.

1 critical _____

2 surgeon _____

3 organ _____

4 마음, 정신 _____

5 윤리적인 _____

6 진퇴양난, 문제 _____

**B** 괄호 안의 주어진 단어를 바르게 배열하시오.

1 Such patients could be (for, organs, transplantation, a source of).

→ _____

2 (kept, all, whose, beating, Not, hearts, those) ever recovered other critical functions.

→ _____

**C** 다음 빈칸에 들어갈 알맞은 단어를 적으시오.

1 그들의 뇌가 완전히 기능하는 것을 멈추었다.

Their brains had _____ to _____ altogether.

2 그 권고는 그 후 일부 수정들과 함께 채택되었다.

The _____ has since _____ _____, with some _____.

**D** 다음 괄호 안의 주어진 단어를 활용하여 문장을 완성하시오.

1 심장 이식을 할 수 있는 능력은 인공호흡기의 개발과 관련이 있었다. (The ability, perform, transplants, link, respirators) 13단어

→ _____

_____

2 모든 식별 가능한 중추 신경계 활동의 부재는 사망의 새로운 기준이 되어야 한다. (The absence, discernible, central nervous system activity, criterion) 16단어

→ _____

_____

**A** 우리말은 영어로, 영어는 우리말로 쓰시오.

1 promote _____

2 muscle mass _____

3 combination _____

4 전략적인 _____

5 간격 _____

6 섭취 _____

**B** 괄호 안의 주어진 단어를 바르게 배열하시오.

1 (no, has, It, on, effect, improving) body composition.

→ _____

2 We can help (much, to, our bodies, faster, heal and grow).

→ _____

**C** 다음 빈칸에 들어갈 알맞은 단어를 적으시오.

1 일시적 유행 다이어트는 여러분을 열량 부족 상태가 되게 할 수도 있다.

Fad diets might _____ you _____ a caloric _____.

2 다량 영양소는 신체가 더 강해지는 능력을 최대화하도록 도와줄 수 있다.

Macronutrients can _____ your body _____ its _____ to grow _____.

**D** 다음 괄호 안의 주어진 단어를 활용하여 문장을 완성하시오.

1 열량 제한은 당신의 에너지 수준을 상당히 감소시킬 수 있다. (Calorie restriction, reduce, significantly) 8단어

→ _____

_____

2 당신의 신체는 치유되기 위해서 주요 다량 영양소의 알맞은 균형도 필요로 한다. (right, key, macronutrients, so as to, heal) 13단어

→ _____

_____

**A** 우리말은 영어로, 영어는 우리말로 쓰시오.

1 immediately _____

2 separate _____

3 as per _____

4 명확한 _____

5 목격하다 _____

6 조금씩, 점차적으로 _____

**B** 괄호 안의 주어진 단어를 바르게 배열하시오.

1 A nurse suggested that (kept together, one incubator, in, be, the twins).

→ _____

2 (Azim, clear, concept, to, became, This) one day when he watched television.

→ _____

**C** 다음 빈칸에 들어갈 알맞은 단어를 적으시오.

1 한 성직자가 갓 태어난 쌍둥이들에 대한 이야기를 들려주었고 그들 중에 한 명은 아팠다.

A _____ was sharing a story about _____ twins, and one of them was ____.

2 이러한 본능적인 교감은 아픈 쌍둥이가 건강을 회복하고 건강을 되찾도록 도와주었다.

This _____ connection helped the sick twin to _____ and to _____ his health.

**D** 다음 괄호 안의 주어진 단어를 활용하여 문장을 완성하시오.

1 건강한 쌍둥이가 즉시 그의 아픈 남동생을 자신의 팔로 감쌌다. (healthy, immediately, put, around) 11단어

→ _____

2 그 의사들은 만질 수 없는 사랑의 힘과 믿을 수 없는 나눔의 힘을 목격하였다. (intangible, force, incredible, power, giving) 14단어

→ _____

**A** 우리말은 영어로, 영어는 우리말로 쓰시오.

1 sign _____

2 heart rate _____

3 confirm _____

4 추적하다 _____

5 암시하다, 추론하다 _____

6 절대로, 분명히 _____

**B** 괄호 안의 주어진 단어를 바르게 배열하시오.

1 (choose, to, valuable, Is, have to, it) between bad and improving?

→ _____

2 She still has to stay in the incubator (stake, is still, since, at, her health).

→ _____

**C** 다음 빈칸에 들어갈 알맞은 단어를 적으시오.

1 그 아기의 건강 상태는 극도로 나쁘다.

The baby's health _____ is _____ bad.

2 그것은 우리가 세계의 현 상태에 관해 생각해야 하는 방식이다.

That is the _____ we must think about the _____ _____ of the world.

**D** 다음 괄호 안의 주어진 단어를 활용하여 문장을 완성하시오.

1 세계를 인큐베이터 안에 있는 미숙아라고 생각해 보라. (Consider, as, premature, incubator) 10단어

→ _____

2 그 아기의 상황이 개선되고 있다고 말하는 것은 이치에 맞는가? (it, make sense, say, that, infant's, improve) 12단어

→ _____

# MINI TEST

Workbook

| MINI TEST 01 |

**A** 우리말은 영어로, 영어는 우리말로 쓰시오.

1  behavior _____

2  restriction _____

3  consequence _____

5  일관성 있는 _____

4  부과하다, 시행하다 _____

6  합당한, 합리적인 _____

**B** 괄호 안의 주어진 단어를 바르게 배열하시오.

1  (behavior, controlled, whose, not, A child, is) improves when clear restrictions are established.

→ _____

2  Effective behavioral change occurs when punishment is linked (the intended, of, to, behavior, praise).

→ _____

**C** 다음 빈칸에 들어갈 알맞은 단어를 적으시오.

1  효과적이려면 부모 양쪽 모두가 제한을 시행해야 한다.

To be _____, both parents have to _____ limits.

2  너무 많은 제한은 배우기 어렵고 자율성의 정상적 발달을 망칠지도 모른다.

Too many limits are difficult to learn and may _____ the normal development of _____.

**D** 다음 괄호 안의 주어진 단어를 활용하여 문장을 완성하시오.

1  부모는 어디에 제한이 설정될지에 대해 (반드시) 합의를 해야 한다. (Parents, agree on, a limit, set) 10단어

→ _____

_____

2  처벌은 간결하고 행동과 직접적으로 관련되어 있어야 한다. (Punishment, must, brief, link, directly) 10단어

→ _____

_____

| MINI TEST 02 |

**A** 우리말은 영어로, 영어는 우리말로 쓰시오.

1  profitable _____

2  retailer _____

3  ecological _____

4  의식, 자각 _____

5  사고방식 _____

6  대안적인 _____

**B** 괄호 안의 주어진 단어를 바르게 배열하시오.

1  A new movement has come to light, (ecological, adding, more, philosophy, a).

→ _____

2  Green Friday (changing, about, the way, is) we see this day and switching our mindset.

→ _____

**C** 다음 빈칸에 들어갈 알맞은 단어를 적으시오.

1  인구의 단지 작은 비율만이 변화를 만든다.

Only a small percentage of the _____ makes the _____.

2  블랙 프라이데이는 휴가 시즌의 시작을 나타내는 일종의 비공식적인 미국의 휴일이었다.

Black Friday has been a sort of _____ U.S. holiday _____ the beginning of the holiday season.

**D** 다음 괄호 안의 주어진 단어를 활용하여 문장을 완성하시오.

1  그린 프라이데이는 그것이 환경에 가져오는 피해에 대한 의식을 높이는 것을 추구한다. (Green Friday, raise, the damage, which) 15단어

→ _____

_____

2  쇼핑몰까지 운전하면서 발생되는 탄소 배출에 대해 생각해 보라. (the carbon emission, which, cause, drive, the mall) 13단어

→ _____

_____

| MINI TEST 03 |

**A 우리말은 영어로, 영어는 우리말로 쓰시오.**

1 fundamental _____

2 emerge _____

3 navigation _____

4 물질 _____

5 사실상 _____

6 인공적인 _____

**B 괄호 안의 주어진 단어를 바르게 배열하시오.**

1 (was, the energy, which, stored, of, Some) in air and water flows was used for navigation.

→ _____

2 This was a fundamental new development, (history, no, were, for which, in, precedents, there).

→ _____

**C 다음 빈칸에 들어갈 알맞은 단어를 적으시오.**

1 인간은 식물을 경작하고 동물을 길들이는 것을 배웠다.

Humans learned to _____ plants and _____ animals.

2 다양한 종류의 기계에 동력을 공급하는 데 화석 연료가 사용되기 시작하였다.

_____ _____ began to be used for _____ machines of different _____.

**D 다음 괄호 안의 주어진 단어를 활용하여 문장을 완성하시오.**

1 우리는 복잡한 형태를 구축한 지구상 유일한 종이다. (this planet, that, have constructed, of complexity) 14단어

→ _____

2 이러한 능력은 150만 년 전에서 50만 년 전 사이에 처음으로 생겨났을지도 모른다. (capacity, may first, emerge, million) 13단어

→ _____

| MINI TEST 04 |

**A 우리말은 영어로, 영어는 우리말로 쓰시오.**

1 line up _____

2 influence _____

3 estimate _____

4 끌어내다, 얻다 _____

5 목격자 _____

6 적대적인 _____

**B 괄호 안의 주어진 단어를 바르게 배열하시오.**

1 (each other, people, influence, to, Allowing) reduces the precision of a group's estimate.

→ _____

2 (an event, are, to, When, multiple witnesses, there), they are not allowed to discuss it.

→ _____

**C 다음 빈칸에 들어갈 알맞은 단어를 적으시오.**

1 이러한 원칙은 좋은 경찰 수사 절차의 일부이다.

This rule is _____ of good _____ _____.

2 그들의 경험을 교환한 목격자들은 비슷한 오류들을 만드는 경향이 있을 것이다.

Witnesses who _____ their experiences will tend to make similar _____.

**D 다음 괄호 안의 주어진 단어를 활용하여 문장을 완성하시오.**

1 당신은 이 출처들을 서로 독립적으로 만들도록 항상 노력해야 한다. (sources, independent of, each other) 13단어

→ _____

2 개방적인 토론의 일반적인 관행은 그들의 의견들에 너무 많은 무게를 실어준다. (standard, practice, open discussion, weight) 13단어

→ _____

| MINI TEST 05 |

**A** 우리말은 영어로, 영어는 우리말로 쓰시오.

1 insight _____

2 conviction _____

3 chaos _____

4 애매모호함 _____

5 질서 _____

6 공식 _____

**B** 괄호 안의 주어진 단어를 바르게 배열하시오.

1 (of, the classic story, Our approach, me, reminds) of the drunk man.

→ _____

2 We stay within our current state, (may, how, no, inferior, be, it, matter).

→ _____

**C** 다음 빈칸에 들어갈 알맞은 단어를 적으시오.

1 우리는 미지의 것과 상호 작용하는 우리의 능력을 잃어버린다.

We lose our _____ to _____ with the _____ .

2 확실성에 대한 우리의 열망은 겉으로 보기에 안전한 해결책을 우리가 추구하도록 이끈다.

Our _____ for _____ leads us to _____ seemingly safe solutions.

**D** 다음 괄호 안의 주어진 단어를 활용하여 문장을 완성하시오.

1 우리는 불확실한 곳에서 확실성을 찾는다.
(look for, uncertain, places) 7단어

→ _____
_____

2 우리는 세상을 통제하려고 하는 것에 훨씬 더 많은 시간과 노력을 쏟는다. (spend, much, effort on, control) 13단어

→ _____

| MINI TEST 06 |

**A** 우리말은 영어로, 영어는 우리말로 쓰시오.

1 attempt _____

2 effortful _____

3 repetition _____

4 (큰) 덩어리 _____

5 유창함, 능변 _____

6 무의식적인, 생각 없는 _____

**B** 괄호 안의 주어진 단어를 바르게 배열하시오.

1 You stop thinking about (it, should, better, how, do, you).

→ _____

2 (which, memorized, of, Each, is, information, chunk) opens up the mental space.

→ _____

**C** 다음 빈칸에 들어갈 알맞은 단어를 적으시오.

1 습관은 숙달의 토대를 만든다.

Habits create the _____ for _____ .

2 당신은 더 높은 수준의 세부 사항에 자유롭게 집중하게 된다.

You are free to _____ _____ _____ more _____ details.

**D** 다음 괄호 안의 주어진 단어를 활용하여 문장을 완성하시오.

1 실수들을 대수롭지 않게 여기기가 더 쉬워진다.
(It, become, let, slide) 7단어

→ _____

2 습관은 그 어떤 탁월함의 추구에 있어서 중추적인 역할을 한다. (Habits, the backbone, any pursuit, excellence) 9단어

→ _____

| MINI TEST 07 |

**A 우리말은 영어로, 영어는 우리말로 쓰시오.**

1 meanwhile _____

2 set ~ aside _____

3 auto repair _____

4 예상치 못하게 _____

5 실망 _____

6 만족한 _____

**B 괄호 안의 주어진 단어를 바르게 배열하시오.**

1 You will (desperate, when, feel, happen, something, does).

→ _____

2 You will have cash to pay for it, and you are (down, paying, still, on, your debt, schedule).

→ _____

**C 다음 빈칸에 들어갈 알맞은 단어를 적으시오.**

1 여러분은 결국 더욱 많은 빚을 지게 될 것이다.

You will _____ _____ _____ _____ into debt.

2 여러분은 모든 여윳돈을 일어날 수도 있는 일을 위해 모아 놓지 않고 빚을 줄이는데 쓴다.

You spend all your extra money _____ debt _____ saving for the things that _____ _____ _____ happen.

**D 다음 괄호 안의 주어진 단어를 활용하여 문장을 완성하시오.**

1 여러분의 차를 수리하기 위해서 예상치 못하게 500달러가 필요하다고 가정해보자. (Let's, unexpectedly, have, repair) 11단어

→ _____

_____

2 여러분은 빚을 갚기 위해 정말 열심히 노력해 왔다는 것에 좌절감을 느끼게 될 것이다. (that, have, be, try, so hard, pay things off) 15단어

→ _____

| MINI TEST 08 |

**A 우리말은 영어로, 영어는 우리말로 쓰시오.**

1 intelligent _____

2 according to _____

3 accomplish _____

4 효율성 _____

5 적응 _____

6 상처[부상] 입은 _____

**B 괄호 안의 주어진 단어를 바르게 배열하시오.**

1 People learn different cultural content and they (similar, with, this, efficiency, accomplish).

→ _____

2 (help, Such, with, particularly, his adaptation, life, to, knowledge, would not) in the East African grasslands.

→ _____

**C 다음 빈칸에 들어갈 알맞은 단어를 적으시오.**

1 사람들은 종종 그가 우리보다 덜 똑똑함이 틀림없다는 것을 당연시한다.

People often _____ _____ _____ _____ that he _____ _____ less intelligent than we _____.

2 그는 3일 동안 본 적 없는 부시벅을 어떻게 추적하는지를 안다.

He knows _____ _____ _____ a bush buck _____ he has not seen _____ three days.

**D 다음 괄호 안의 주어진 단어를 활용하여 문장을 완성하시오.**

1 어떤 문화의 사람들이 빠른 학습자라는 증거는 없다. (There, that, from some cultures, fast learners) 12단어

→ _____

_____

2 그는 생존 기술이 부족했기 때문에 목초지의 환경에 적응하는데 실패했다. (adjust, the environment of the grasslands, short of survival skills) 17단어

→ _____

## | MINI TEST 01 |

**A** 우리말은 영어로, 영어는 우리말로 쓰시오.

1 rim _____
2 still _____
3 disappointed _____
4 기준 _____
5 이전의 _____
6 이런 점에서 _____

**B** 괄호 안의 주어진 단어를 바르게 배열하시오.

1 Basketball games are not (about, criteria, such, pretty or ugly, as).
→ _____

2 The ball hits one side of the rim, (second, a, still, for, rolls around, half, and stands).
→ _____

**C** 다음 빈칸에 들어갈 알맞은 단어를 적으시오.

1 이제 다시 그 똑같은 선수가 또 (다른) 15피트 슛을 한다고 상상해 보자.
_____ _____ _____ that same player _____ another fifteen-foot _____.

2 만약 당신이 "완벽한" 대신에 "완수된"을 삽입한다면 완벽함은 실제로 가능하다.
_____ actually is possible _____ you insert "complete" _____ _____ "perfect."

**D** 다음 괄호 안의 주어진 단어를 활용하여 문장을 완성하시오.

1 당신이 완벽하다는 것에 대한 다른 관점이 필요하다. (another, perspective of, perfect) 7단어
→ _____
_____

2 사람들은 그것이 "완벽한" 슛이 아니라서 실망할 수도 있다. (might, disappoint, that, a "perfect" shot) 11단어
→ _____

## | MINI TEST 02 |

**A** 우리말은 영어로, 영어는 우리말로 쓰시오.

1 acquire _____
2 component _____
3 emission _____
4 경작 _____
5 요인, 동인 _____
6 ~을 절제하다, 삼가다 _____

**B** 괄호 안의 주어진 단어를 바르게 배열하시오.

1 The transport and grain cultivation associated (with, industry, the livestock, the main, drivers, are).
→ _____

2 How can we acquire the nutrients we need (the environment, with, damaged, less)?
→ _____

**C** 다음 빈칸에 들어갈 알맞은 단어를 적으시오.

1 기후 변화에 기여하는 것은 가축이다.
It is livestock that _____ _____ climate change.

2 육우와 젖소는 세계의 이산화탄소 배출의 41%를 차지한다.
Beef cattle and milk cattle _____ _____ 41% of the world's $CO_2$ emissions.

**D** 다음 괄호 안의 주어진 단어를 활용하여 문장을 완성하시오.

1 식량 체계가 야기하는 지구 온난화 가능성은 상당히 줄어들 것이다. (The chance, that, the food system, would, substantially, reduce) 14단어
→ _____
_____

2 전통적인 가축과 대조하여, 곤충들은 재배된 곡물보다는 음식물 쓰레기를 먹고 살 수 있다. (In contrast, conventional, live on, rather than) 15단어
→ _____
_____

| MINI TEST 03 |

**A** 우리말은 영어로, 영어는 우리말로 쓰시오.

1 absurd _____

2 depression _____

3 be obsessed with _____

4 희박한, 드문 _____

5 편견 _____

6 위암 _____

**B** 괄호 안의 주어진 단어를 바르게 배열하시오.

1 (of, us, fear, the victims, being, a, is, There) of a plane crash.

→ _____

2 (It, travel through, we, that, an incorrect, likely, life, is, with) risk map in our heads.

→ _____

**C** 다음 빈칸에 들어갈 알맞은 단어를 적으시오.

1 우리는 가장 쉽게 마음속에 떠오르는 것과 세상에 대한 이미지를 연관시켜 생각한다.

We _____ an image of the world _____ _____ most easily comes to mind.

2 우리가 쉽게 떠올리는 것은 사건들이 얼마나 자주 발생하는지와 아무 관련이 없다.

_____ we can easily recall _____ _____ _____ _____ _____ how frequently things happen.

**D** 다음 괄호 안의 주어진 단어를 활용하여 문장을 완성하시오.

1 폭탄 공격의 가능성은 우리가 생각하는 것보다 훨씬 더 희박하다. (The chances, attacks, much) **11단어**

→ _____

_____

2 우리는 당뇨병과 같은 덜 눈에 띄는 방법으로 죽을 위험성을 간과한다. (overlook, die from, noticeable, means, such as, diabetes) **16단어**

→ _____

_____

| MINI TEST 04 |

**A** 우리말은 영어로, 영어는 우리말로 쓰시오.

1 honor _____

2 set out _____

3 circumstances _____

4 다루다 _____

5 적용하다 _____

6 닿다, 이르다 _____

**B** 괄호 안의 주어진 단어를 바르게 배열하시오.

1 A cat in a tiny box will behave like a fluid, (the, filling up, space, all).

→ _____

2 Whether cats are liquid or solid is the kind of (earn, question, a Nobel Prize, that, could).

→ _____

**C** 다음 빈칸에 들어갈 알맞은 단어를 적으시오.

1 고양이들은 그들이 들어가 앉아 있는 용기의 모양에 적응할 수 있다.

Cats can _____ _____ the shape of the _____ they sit in.

2 그는 고양이가 욕조의 공간에 자리를 잡는데 걸리는 시간을 계산했다.

He calculated the time _____ _____ _____ cats _____ settle down in the space of a bathroom sink.

**D** 다음 괄호 안의 주어진 단어를 활용하여 문장을 완성하시오.

1 고양이들은 환경에 따라 액체나 고체 둘 중 하나가 될 수 있다. (either, depend on, the circumstances) **11단어**

→ _____

_____

2 욕조 안의 고양이는 물이 그것(고양이)에게 닿는 것을 막으려고 노력할 것이다. (A cat in a bathtub, prevent, reach) **13단어**

→ _____

_____

| MINI TEST 05 |

**A** 우리말은 영어로, 영어는 우리말로 쓰시오.

1 chemical _____

2 burst _____

3 release _____

4 우월(성) _____

5 저항하는 _____

6 질투하는 _____

**B** 괄호 안의 주어진 단어를 바르게 배열하시오.

1 Some kinds of addictions (result, or, manic behavior, could).

→ _____

2 We do not realize the role (plays, in, such, hard-earned gains, luck, that).

→ _____

**C** 다음 빈칸에 들어갈 알맞은 단어를 적으시오.

1 우리는 많은 돈을 얻는 것으로부터 그런 기쁨을 되찾으려고 노력한다.

We try to recapture that _____ from _____ a lot of money.

2 그들은 필연적인 추락을 경험하는데, 그것은 훨씬 더 고통스럽다.

They _____ an inevitable fall, which is much more _____.

**D** 다음 괄호 안의 주어진 단어를 활용하여 문장을 완성하시오.

1 이익들이 빠르게 올 때, 우리는 기본적인 지혜를 잊어버리는 경향이 있다. (gains, tend, sight, basic) 13단어

→ _____
_____

2 필연적인 추락은 주기(사이클)의 우울 부분으로 이어진다. (fall, lead, the depression part) 11단어

→ _____
_____

| MINI TEST 06 |

**A** 우리말은 영어로, 영어는 우리말로 쓰시오.

1 effort _____

2 patient _____

3 completely _____

4 사라지다 _____

5 사실, 실은, 실제로 _____

6 계속하다, 수행하다 _____

**B** 괄호 안의 주어진 단어를 바르게 배열하시오.

1 A man tries (by, to make, a fire, rubbing) two sticks of wood together.

→ _____

2 He becomes more and more (he, until, discouraged, gives up completely).

→ _____

**C** 다음 빈칸에 들어갈 알맞은 단어를 적으시오.

1 즉각적으로 일어나는 것은 없으므로, 우리는 처음에는 어떤 결과들도 볼 수 없다.

_____ happens immediately, so we can't _____ any results at first.

2 그 열은 사라져버렸는데, 그가 충분히 오랫동안 계속하지 않았기 때문이다.

The heat has _____, since he didn't continue for long _____.

**D** 다음 괄호 안의 주어진 단어를 활용하여 문장을 완성하시오.

1 그는 의욕을 잃게 되고 잠시 쉬려고 멈춘다. (get, rest, while) 10단어

→ _____
_____

2 그는 그 일을 하고 있었지만, 불이 생길 만큼의 충분한 열이 없었다. (but, there, start a fire) 14단어

→ _____
_____

**| MINI TEST 07 |**

**A** 우리말은 영어로, 영어는 우리말로 쓰시오.

1 intensity     _____

2 operate     _____

3 process     _____

4 순응, 적응     _____

5 ~에 익숙한     _____

6 신맛이 나는     _____

**B** 괄호 안의 주어진 단어를 바르게 배열하시오.

1 Place one hand in hot water (iced water, the other, and, in).

→ _____

2 Intensity is coded and relativity (to control, operates, our, sensations).

→ _____

**C** 다음 빈칸에 들어갈 알맞은 단어를 적으시오.

1 상대적인 증가와 감소는 뉴런이 신호를 보내는 속도로 작동한다.

A _____ increase or decrease works in the rate \_\_\_\_ _____ the neurons fire.

2 그것은 또한 달콤한 초콜릿을 먹은 후에 사과가 신맛이 나는 이유를 설명해 준다.

It also _____ the reason apples _____ sour after eating sweet chocolate.

**D** 다음 괄호 안의 주어진 단어를 활용하여 문장을 완성하시오.

1 당신은 온도의 상충하는(서로 다른) 감각들을 경험할 것이다. (conflicting sensations, temperature) 7단어

→ _____

_____

2 일단 당신이 햇볕이 쨍쨍한 날에 내부로 들어왔을 때 당신은 어두운 방 안에서 눈이 멀게 된다. (get, inside, once, have, from) 16단어

→ _____

_____

**| MINI TEST 08 |**

**A** 우리말은 영어로, 영어는 우리말로 쓰시오.

1 term     _____

2 device     _____

3 rapid     _____

4 흡입     _____

5 언급, 참고, 지침     _____

6 언급하다, 말하다     _____

**B** 괄호 안의 주어진 단어를 바르게 배열하시오.

1 The term "vacuum" used (name, is, for, an, this device, inappropriate).

→ _____

2 (references, to find, It, is, hard, any) to "vacuum" prior to Booth.

→ _____

**C** 다음 빈칸에 들어갈 알맞은 단어를 적으시오.

1 그는 '진공청소기'라는 용어를 만든 최초의 사람이라고 주장했을 뿐이었다.

He only _____ to be the first to coin the term "_____ cleaner."

2 그는 그의 의도된 발명품을 설명한 임시 제품 설명서를 제출했다.

He _____ a provisional specification _____ his intended invention.

**D** 다음 괄호 안의 주어진 단어를 활용하여 문장을 완성하시오.

1 그것은 폐쇄된 용기 속으로 작은 구멍을 통해 유입되는 공기이다. (move, through, into, close, container) 13단어

→ _____

_____

2 흥미롭게도, Booth 자신도 '진공'이라는 용어를 언급하지 않았다. (Booth himself, the term "vacuum") 9단어

→ _____

_____

| MINI TEST 01 |

**A** 우리말은 영어로, 영어는 우리말로 쓰시오.

1 tension _____

2 passive _____

3 spectator _____

4 중요한, 시사하는 _____

5 표현하다 _____

6 추구하다 _____

**B** 괄호 안의 주어진 단어를 바르게 배열하시오.

1 Recreation meets (wide range, individual, a, needs, of) and interests.

→ _____

2 Other significant play motivations (creativity, on, the need, to express, are based).

→ _____

**C** 다음 빈칸에 들어갈 알맞은 단어를 적으시오.

1 그들은 텔레비전을 즐기는 여흥의 수동적 구경꾼일지도 모른다.

They may be _____ spectators of entertainment who _____ television.

2 그것은 때때로 그들이 다른 사람들이나 환경에 투쟁하도록 돕는다.

It sometimes helps them _____ against others or the _____.

**D** 다음 괄호 안의 주어진 단어를 활용하여 문장을 완성하시오.

1 많은 참여자들은 휴식의 형태로 레크리에이션에 참여한다. (Many, take part in, form, relaxation) 11단어

→ _____

_____

2 레크리에이션은 매우 사교적이고 새로운 친구들을 만들 기회를 제공한다. (highly, social, and, provide, the opportunity for) 13단어

→ _____

_____

| MINI TEST 02 |

**A** 우리말은 영어로, 영어는 우리말로 쓰시오.

1 exact _____

2 origin _____

3 pottery _____

4 모조(품); 가짜의 _____

5 탐구하다, 탐험하다 _____

6 원동력, 추진력 _____

**B** 괄호 안의 주어진 단어를 바르게 배열하시오.

1 It can (difficult, their, be, to know) exact origins.

→ _____

2 Archaeologists will find even (in, the future, older, pots, somewhere else).

→ _____

**C** 다음 빈칸에 들어갈 알맞은 단어를 적으시오.

1 때때로 과학자들은 초기 발명품의 모형을 발견한다.

From time to time scientists _____ a model of an _____ invention.

2 고고학자들은 도자기가 근동지역에서 처음 발명되었다고 믿었다.

Archaeologists believed _____ was first _____ in the Near East.

**D** 다음 괄호 안의 주어진 단어를 활용하여 문장을 완성하시오.

1 많은 발명품들은 수천 년 전에 창조되었다. (Many, create, of, ago) 8단어

→ _____

_____

2 다른 과학자들은 똑같은 발명품의 훨씬 더 오래된 모형들을 발견할 것이다. (discover, even, old) 11단어

→ _____

_____

## | MINI TEST 03 |

**A** 우리말은 영어로, 영어는 우리말로 쓰시오.

1 nearly     _____

2 actually     _____

3 noticeable     _____

4 정도     _____

5 추정하다     _____

6 자극하여 ~하게 하다     _____

**B** 괄호 안의 주어진 단어를 바르게 배열하시오.

1 The spotlight effect is (in which, at center stage, we, see, the, ourselves, phenomenon).

→ _____

2 He researched the spotlight effect (into, having, a sweatshirt, college, by, change, students).

→ _____

**C** 다음 빈칸에 들어갈 알맞은 단어를 적으시오.

1 우리는 다른 사람들이 우리에게 관심을 기울이는 정도를 자연스럽게 과대평가한다.

We naturally overestimate the extent _____ _____ others _____ _____ _____ us.

2 그들 중 거의 40 퍼센트가 다른 학생들이 셔츠에 무엇이 있었는지 기억할 것이라고 확신했다.

_____ 40 percent of them _____ sure the other students would remember _____ _____ on the shirt.

**D** 다음 괄호 안의 주어진 단어를 활용하여 문장을 완성하시오.

1 그 학생들은 몇 분 동안 방을 떠난 후에 운동복 상의들을 갈아입었다. (sweatshirts, after, a few) 12단어

→ _____

_____

2 두드러지는 옷들조차도 오직 23 퍼센트의 관찰자들만이 알아차리게 했다. (noticeable, provoke, notice) 11단어

→ _____

_____

## | MINI TEST 04 |

**A** 우리말은 영어로, 영어는 우리말로 쓰시오.

1 declare     _____

2 advocate     _____

3 contemporary     _____

4 사소한     _____

5 엄격히     _____

6 검열하다     _____

**B** 괄호 안의 주어진 단어를 바르게 배열하시오.

1 The Catholic Church strictly (controlled, could, what, be, published).

→ _____

2 (of, censored, Many, Voltaire's books, were) and burned publicly.

→ _____

**C** 다음 빈칸에 들어갈 알맞은 단어를 적으시오.

1 어떤 사소한 의견도 들려질 자격이 있다.

Any _____ opinion _____ _____ be heard.

2 이 중 아무것도 그가 편견과 가식에 도전하는 것을 멈추게 하지 못했다.

_____ of this _____ him _____ challenging the _____ and pretensions.

**D** 다음 괄호 안의 주어진 단어를 활용하여 문장을 완성하시오.

1 그는 종교적 신념을 조롱한 이유로 다시 감옥에 갇혔을 것이다. (have, imprison, for, beliefs) 13단어

→ _____

_____

2 나는 여러분이 하는 말을 싫어하지만 그것을 말할 여러분의 권리를 옹호할 것이다. (what, defend, right) 13단어

→ _____

_____

| MINI TEST 05 |

**A** 우리말은 영어로, 영어는 우리말로 쓰시오.

1  enrich _____

2  laborer _____

3  construct _____

4  장애물 _____

5  우아함 _____

6  점진적으로 _____

**B** 괄호 안의 주어진 단어를 바르게 배열하시오.

1  (Today, don't, you, necessarily, What, do, have to), put off until tomorrow.

→ _____

2  Time (to, in a day, be, is, meant, not, spent), but consumed without hurry.

→ _____

**C** 다음 빈칸에 들어갈 알맞은 단어를 적으시오.

1  결정을 내리는 것을 미루는 것이 그 자체로 하나의 결정이다.

To put off _____ a _____ is _____ a decision.

2  만약 당신이 아이디어와 결정을 미룬다면, 그것들은 당연히 향상될 것이다.

If you _____ your ideas and decisions, they _____ _____ improve.

**D** 다음 괄호 안의 주어진 단어를 활용하여 문장을 완성하시오.

1  그 정치적 과정은 본질적으로 미루기와 협의의 체계이다. (essentially, a system, deliberation) 11단어

→ _____

_____

2  건축가들과 일꾼들이 Blenheim 궁전을 건설하는데 15년이 걸렸다. (It, take, construct, Palace) 11단어

→ _____

_____

| MINI TEST 06 |

**A** 우리말은 영어로, 영어는 우리말로 쓰시오.

1  instantly _____

2  organism _____

3  physiological _____

4  수정(하기) _____

5  만성적인 _____

6  발전되다, 진화하다 _____

**B** 괄호 안의 주어진 단어를 바르게 배열하시오.

1  However, (science, that, way, work, actually, doesn't).

→ _____

2  Biological breakthrough has changed (how, our, the human, organism, understanding of, works).

→ _____

**C** 다음 빈칸에 들어갈 알맞은 단어를 적으시오.

1  '획기적인 발견'이라는 말은 놀랍고 새로운 발견을 의미하는 것처럼 보인다.

The word "breakthrough" _____ _____ _____ an amazing, _____ discovery.

2  획기적인 발견은 과학자들의 연구를 기반으로 하여 그러한 방식으로 일어났다.

The breakthrough _____ in that _____, _____ _____ the _____ of _____.

**D** 다음 괄호 안의 주어진 단어를 활용하여 문장을 완성하시오.

1  그 연구가 진행되는 만큼 그 이야기는 계속 발전된다. (to, evolve, as, go on) 10단어

→ _____

_____

2  당신은 초등학교 때, 여러분이 처음 배웠던 과학적 방법을 기억하는가? (method, first learn, when in elementary school) 14단어

→ _____

_____

| MINI TEST 07 |

**A 우리말은 영어로, 영어는 우리말로 쓰시오.**

1 transfer      _____

2 molecule      _____

3 loudness      _____

4 밀도      _____

5 요소      _____

6 음파      _____

**B 괄호 안의 주어진 단어를 바르게 배열하시오.**

1 Then, (your, ear, top, place, close, the table, of, to).

   → _____

2 (your finger, With, from your ear, about, one foot, away), tap the table top.

   → _____

**C 다음 빈칸에 들어갈 알맞은 단어를 적으시오.**

1 고체 속의 분자들이 공기 중의 그것들보다 훨씬 더 가깝고 더 집중되어 있다.

   The _____ in solids are much _____ and more _____ than _____ in the air.

2 음파는 공기를 통해서 뿐만 아니라 많은 고체 물질을 통해 이동할 수 있다.

   Sound waves can travel _____ many solid materials _____ _____ _____ through the air.

**D 다음 괄호 안의 주어진 단어를 활용하여 문장을 완성하시오.**

1 책상 위에 귀를 대고 당신이 듣는 그 소리가 훨씬 더 크다. (The sound, with your ear, the, much) 13단어

   → _____

2 공기의 밀도가 음파의 소리 크기를 결정하는 요소로 작용한다. (The density, play, a determining factor, the loudness, the sound waves) 16단어

   → _____

| MINI TEST 08 |

**A 우리말은 영어로, 영어는 우리말로 쓰시오.**

1 shape      _____

2 describe      _____

3 objective      _____

4 상대적으로      _____

5 우연한      _____

6 비교      _____

**B 괄호 안의 주어진 단어를 바르게 배열하시오.**

1 Leon Festinger's theory describes (how other people, are, you, shape who).

   → _____

2 The self is formed by social environment, (as, looking, by, well, as inwards, outwards).

   → _____

**C 다음 빈칸에 들어갈 알맞은 단어를 적으시오.**

1 물론 이러한 사실은 객관적이지도 고정된 것도 아니다.

   These facts are _____ objective _____ fixed, of course.

2 의심할 바 없이 당신은 상대적으로 수학을 못한다고 느낄 것이다.

   _____ _____ you feel that you're relatively _____ _____ math.

**D 다음 괄호 안의 주어진 단어를 활용하여 문장을 완성하시오.**

1 이러한 사회적 비교들은 완전히 우연한 것이 아니다. (aren't, entirely) 6단어

   → _____

2 긍정적인 면을 본다면, 당신은 춤을 더 잘 춘다고 느낄지도 모른다. (Looking, the bright side, like, better) 14단어

   → _____

MEMO

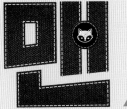

수능 영어를 향한 가벼운 발걸음

# 맨처음 수능 영어

## 주제별 독해 2

## Workbook

★ 정답률 높은 기출 문제만을 선별

★ 모의고사 및 수능 기출 지문을 쉽게 변형

★ 수능 빈출 소재 & 주제별 학습으로 수능 독해력 향상

★ 전 지문 워크북 문제 제공으로 반복 복습 및 응용 학습 가능

QR코드를 통해 본 교재의 상세 정보와 MP3 파일 및 부가학습 자료를 이용하실 수 있습니다.

# 수능 영어를 향한 가벼운 발걸음
# 맨처음 수능 영어 시리즈

○ 정답률 높은 기출 문제만 선별
○ 모의고사 및 수능 기출 지문을 쉽게 변형
○ 수능 유형 학습에서 수능 실전 감각까지 익히는 체계적인 단계별 학습
○ 전 지문 워크북 문제 제공으로 반복 복습 및 응용 학습 가능

---

**유형 학습**

## 수능 대표 유형으로 첫 마스터!

• 수능 대표 유형 소개와 유형별 학습 방향 제시
• 유형별 문제풀이 전략과 오답을 피하는 생생한 팁 제공

입문편 13,000원 | 기본편, 실력편 각 14,500원

---

**주제별 학습**

## 수능 주제별 학습으로 독해력 향상하기!

• 수능 빈출 소재 & 주제별 학습 방향 제시
• 주제별 다양한 배경지식과 풍부한 어휘 학습 제공

주제별 독해 1, 2 각 14,500원

---

**모의고사 학습**

## 수능형 모의고사로 실전 감각 키우기!

• 쉬운 어휘로 모의고사 및 수능 기출 문제 풀이
• 수능 시험과 동일한 구성으로 실전 훈련 가능

독해 모의고사 10회 15,000원 | 완성편(듣기+독해) 14,000원

---

**문법 학습**

## 수능 영문법을 개념과 문제풀이로 끝내기!

• 고등학생을 위한 수능 필수 문법 집중 학습
• 최신 수능 유형에 맞춘 수능 기반 내신 문법 첫 마스터
• 개념이해책과 문제풀이책 연계 학습으로 어법 파악 능력 향상

수능 영문법 개념이해책, 문제풀이책 각 13,000원